Some Call It Heresy

Some Call It Heresy

Martin Weber

REVIEW AND HERALD PUBLISHING ASSOCIATION
Washington, DC 20039-0555
Hagerstown, MD 21740

Editor: Raymond H. Woolsey
Book design: Richard Steadham

Unless otherwise noted, all Scripture quotations are from the *New American Standard Bible,* © The Lockman Foundation 1960, 1962, 1963, 1968, 1971, 1972, 1973, 1975, 1977.

Scripture quotations marked Amplified are from the *Amplified New Testament,* © The Lockman Foundation 1954, 1958.

Texts credited to N.E.B. are from *The New English Bible.* © The Delegates of the Oxford University Press and the Syndics of the Cambridge University Press 1961, 1970. Reprinted by permission.

Texts credited to N.I.V. are from *The Holy Bible: New International Version.* Copyright © 1978 by the International Bible Society. Used by permission of Zondervan Bible Publishers.

Scripture quotations marked R.S.V. in this publication are from the Revised Standard Version of the Bible, copyrighted 1946, 1952 © 1971, 1973.

Library of Congress Cataloging in Publication Data
Weber, Martin E.
    Some call it heresy.

    1. Seventh-day Adventists—Apologetic works.
I. Title.
BX6154.W423   1984   230'.6732   85-8344
ISBN 0-8280-0248-7

Printed in U.S.A.

Contents

Foreword

The clear, joyous ring of positive Christian assurance that this book brings to its readers is refreshing to me personally. Before you turn the page, please let me tell you why I feel this way.

I have always been a firm believer in the authority and validity of the gift of prophecy as manifested in the Seventh-day Adventist Church through the writings of Ellen G. White. Recently there have been demands for a reappraisal of this gift. That reappraisal has further clarified and strengthened my confidence in the writings.

I believe that the church understands more clearly now the fundamental nature of divine inspiration as it relates to the life and work of Ellen White. This understanding has been a stabilizing factor in the minds of many as we move into the time when all points of the message will be controverted.

Perhaps the one most helpful feature of this clarification of the work of Ellen White is simply that her gift was not designed as a substitute for sound personal Bible study. Her visions and counsels were not the origin or the sole support of the teachings of the church she loved. Rather, the Spirit of God led the pioneers of the Adventist Church to persevere in searching the Word of God to discover its fundamental teachings. Our unique message is not a debtor to the "gift" for its origin, but rather the result of the Spirit's approval following painstaking study of the Scriptures.

It is precisely for this reason that I've been following with deepening interest Martin Weber's development of this book's manuscript for the past three years. I've been impressed with the way his delightful pen has highlighted his own grasp of the end-time truth of the judgment as found solely in the Word of God. And now that his Scripture conclusions are found to be in harmony with the "gift," it has not surprised me in the least.

A careful reading of this book will prove richly rewarding to the honest seeker for truth.

George E. Vandeman

1 My Brush With "Omega"

Why me, Lord? Why now?"

I was concluding my first season as evangelist for an eastern conference of the Seventh-day Adventist Church. Anticipating satisfaction from a year's hard labor, my heart was stunned instead with bewilderment and frustration. Enthusiastically I had proclaimed the Seventh-day Adventist Church to be God's final remnant, founded upon Scripture alone. On this Biblical basis I invited audiences to unite with my church. I even solemnly affirmed that if any of our teachings were not totally scriptural, I would leave Adventism immediately, despite my deep love for my church. This claim was an effective clincher that moved believers into baptism.

Now I wished I could hide from my bold assertion. It appeared that I had to choose between living in hypocrisy and leaving my beloved church. The problem arose from our celebrated doctrinal Gibraltar, the three angels' messages of Revelation 14. Specifically, the point that perplexed me in this passage was the heavenly sanctuary judgment that precedes the coming of Christ.

Being fully convinced of the judgment's legitimacy, I never expected to doubt this landmark pillar of faith in Jesus. After all, concepts from the sanctuary had been woven into my earliest religious instruction—with some unpleasant results, I must admit.

Frozen Buds of First Faith

As a tot in kindergarten, for example, I was dutifully notified that the Lord could transport only the good and pure to the Holy City. My young conscience assured me that I did not qualify, so fear of Christ's disfavor froze the buds of first faith.

The dedicated teachers of church school brought me benefit in many ways. Unfortunately, despite their Christian commitment and love for me, they succeeded only in darkening the gloom of spiritual insecurity that already hung over my young soul. They exhorted me to be constantly confessing my sins so the angel could erase the black marks that marred my page in the book of judgment. If I died with a spot upon my record, God's justice would certainly consign me to hell.

Teenagers are notorious for sowing wild oats. In their genuine concern for us, our academy instructors faithfully (yet futilely) worked to weed out our adolescent follies with a compilation of threats from the throne of grace. We were taught that soon earth's probation would close, when the Lord would cease working for His people and begin scrutinizing us instead. If our celestial report card revealed anything less than absolute perfection we would be lost, they warned us, loud and clear.

With the forbidden lusts afforded by adolescence seldom out of sight or mind, this blessed state of perfection seemed far out of reach. At least until the overripe age of 30. Worse yet, the awesome investigation of Christian character had begun in 1844 with the cases of the dead and might even now be evaluating those unfortunate enough to be alive. My doom could be sealed before I knew it! And this was the "good news" of the remnant church that was supposed to brighten up the whole earth!

As an academy senior I confessed my dismal record of failure and tried once more to qualify as a Christian. Yet even though I begged for Christ's strength to carry me past the need for forgiveness, utter frustration mocked my faith. Soon that web of discouragement imprisoned me again. Finally, reluctantly, I allowed the world to rescue me from religion.

In the autumn of 1969 I enrolled as a psychology major at Columbia Union College near Washington, D.C. Religion being now a nonevent for me, my only concessions to a restless conscience were regular church attendance and the tithe tax. I did not regard salvation as a reasonable option, and therefore I ignored the Lord. When I became a sophomore, however, the guilt became unmanageable. I repented in October during the Week of Spiritual Emphasis.

Marching as to War

This time around, being especially determined to succeed as a Christian, I vigorously plucked off sin's dead leaves. But soon legalism hijacked my sincerity and began breaking off life's innocent branches. Then the inevitable happened—fanaticism captured me at a weekend retreat for students. The guest speaker taught that my mistakes were keeping the Lord in His sanctuary. Christ was even now experiencing terrible pain—He was being crucified afresh every time I failed in my attempts to please Him. His agony would not cease until all the remnant are absolutely perfect in character, able to pass the investigative judgment without benefit of His blood to cover sinfulness. Not until then would we be fit to pass through the time of trouble without His mediation. Finally He could close probation and take us up to heaven.

Words cannot describe the trauma this sanctuary teaching brought to me. I could not rest day or night, tormented by my conscience because of my sinfulness. The belief that after a lifelong struggle to please God I would be condemned to hell for a minute's shortcoming drove me into ceaseless and useless sacrifice. With frequent fasting and incessant soul-searching I begged God to stop my failures so I would not be guilty of crucifying Jesus anew every time I stumbled.

Yet still I kept sinning. Nothing big, really—just that general imperfection of our fallen human condition in coming short of God's glorious ideal. Why, oh, why could I find no joy in Jesus? Someone admonished me to search my heart again for some secret sin that must be obstructing the Holy Spirit. But what was left? I repented of Christian dating and Saturday night socials. Next came fervent health "reform." Still I found no satisfaction—even after giving up dairy products! Finally I abandoned the college that permitted such "abominations."

The summer of 1972 found me leading a group of student literature evangelists in Appalachia. Vigorously I taught my team the ways of holiness, winning respect but not discipleship—they called me "the fellow that never smiles." Amazingly, despite my depressing leadership, a sincere company of Sabbathkeepers was raised up.

Soon I was called to be lay pastor in a small mining town. Providentially, the brethren picked the right man for the job—because the church had long been closed, I could not do much damage there. With the sanctuary doctrine the heart of my "Christ-centered" theology, I was zealously preaching "righteousness by faith" when a letter arrived from the conference office. Word had reached the president of my legalistic doctrine and fanatic lifestyle. He was alarmed. In tactful terms he warned me that my "spiritual growth" needed to be "much in evidence" before November, when my progress was due for review. The implication was clear—my ministry was on the verge of oblivion.

What a crushing blow! Now, looking back, I understand. Something had to be done about me.

Placed Under a Rest

Before my probation closed in November, a new conference president arrived who understood my sincerity, and he extended my opportunity. He took pity on my misplaced zeal in competing with the accomplishments of Christ, encouraging me to accept our Saviour's victories as if I had achieved them myself. For the first time I saw the light. Finally the truth had come to set me free. After a life of struggle and despair, my troubled heart found rest at the cross.

My growing confidence in salvation was closely paralleled by enlarged attendance in the churches under my care. Two congregations were resurrected, then a larger city district became my ministry. This church also experienced unexpected growth as many welcomed liberation from legalism.

About this time another administration moved into office. After ordaining me to the gospel ministry, they selected me as their conference evangelist. In February of 1979 I sallied forth to win converts to Christ and His truth with my Revelation Lectures.

God graciously blessed the meetings, and by August some of the more fruitful campaigns in recent memory were conducted. My fondest aspirations seemed within reach. Daily I praised God for triumph both in conscience and ministry.

The darkness was past and bright sunlight had come to stay, I thought. Then suddenly the fog moved in.

I could not comprehend it. Seven years earlier I had left college because of my convictions on the sanctuary. My memory was still sore from five years before, when my fanaticism on this teaching had nearly crushed my career. Now it seemed once more that I might lose my ministry over this same doctrine—from an opposite perspective. How could it happen?

Affair With "Omega"

Several young pastors in our conference had rejected the prophetic platform of Adventism because of the pre-Advent judgment. Everything was fulfilled at the cross, they insisted. Christ intended to come in the first century, not eighteen hundred years later. They also contended that Adventist sanctuary theology is nonscriptural, resting instead on the writings of Ellen G. White.

Concerned that their theology might comprise the dreaded "omega" heresy warned against by Ellen White, I contested, but I could not immediately disprove their positions from Scripture. Before long the conference officials became worried about them, so I considered avoiding further study with them. Why risk being identified as a dissident? Anyway, I cherished my job, and it fed my family. Having barely survived previous controversy on the sanctuary, I did not relish new debate.

But perhaps, I thought, these young preachers needed me to help them achieve doctrinal balance and remain loyal to the church. Besides, it seemed other preachers wanted to talk about cars and sports or discuss personalities and methods. These guys actually studied the Bible together. They even promised to consider my objections to their theology.

I had always tried to be a patriot of truth. Although I treasured both the favor of God and the long-delayed favor of man, the former meant more than the latter. So I decided to study with them and ignore the risk. After all, we Adventists constantly remind fellow Christians that truth has nothing to hide from the Bible.

Never before did I enjoy such brotherhood. We would rent a motel room before workers' meetings and search the Scriptures together until past midnight. But the joy did not last. I soon received a request from the president to cease this study of "out-of-the-mainstream" theology. I agreed to his directive, but suggested that something might be wrong with the "mainstream" because Christ had not yet come. I confessed to having serious doubts myself about Adventist doctrine and informed him that my conscience required a definite Biblical base for belief. Even if the church disagreed.

In retrospect, I feel that our little "gospel" group had developed a we-versus-they mentality that may have bordered on arrogance. Perhaps if we had humbly worked to bridge the widening gap between ourselves and administration, unity and mutual tolerance could have been won. Instead, we fostered an ominous atmosphere of suspicion. Despite our sincerity, this was inexcusable. (By God's grace I finally recovered and survived, but the others eventually resigned or were removed from the Adventist ministry.)

What a terrible dilemma confronted me at this point! Must I leave my beloved church? But why belong to a denomination, anyway? All year long I had told audiences that the only basis for membership is totally scriptural teaching. Now could I be a hypocrite myself?

Night after night these questions harassed my heart. How cruel! This was to be a time of rejoicing, the celebration of a harvest. Throughout the State people were resting in the Advent hope, and I who had led them there was writhing in the valley of decision. For the first time in years I became depressed. Bitterness began to strangle my loyalty to denominational leadership. My mind needed to know: If we are the Biblical remnant, somebody please answer from the Bible this challenge to our church. Why this scriptural silence?* Are the heretics correct after all? Why could I not brush this controversy aside as others had done?

But throughout this personal Gethsemane, I knew that the decision had been made already. Nine years earlier, in fact, when I gave my life to Jesus. I would follow truth wherever God led.

At this point the president was thoroughly alarmed. He arranged for me to be escorted by the Ministerial director to the White Estate to regain my doctrinal moorings. I was touched by the kindness and attempts at helpfulness that met me there, but I remained determined to resign unless the church could sustain its claim of being based upon *sola scriptura*—the Bible and the Bible only.

Born-again Again

God was very close to me in this time of trouble. Not through neglecting prayer was I in this dilemma. Indeed, never before had I prayed more earnestly. Through His guiding hand I attended the winter quarter at the Seminary extention of Andrews University held in Hinsdale, Illinois. In Mark Finley, the director of the institute, I met someone who was willing and able to defend from Scripture the Adventist doctrine on the sanctuary. I grew to respect Mark as a loving friend and honest Bible student who was afraid of no question. He determined to help me find answers, and he did.

At Hinsdale I was reborn into the Adventist faith. When the invitation came to pastor the Anaheim church in California, I was able to respond as an enthusiastic soldier of Christ in this church.

This book explains why I remain a Seventh-day Adventist. I pray that each reader will share my confidence in Christ and in the treasures of truth He gave to this movement of destiny. Friends who left the ministry may question my motives for remaining an Adventist, but God knows my heart. I invite them and anyone else who has given up on the church to look over my shoulder at the points made in the chapters that follow.

---

* Since my struggle in 1979, many excellent articles have been published in the *Adventist Review* and *Ministry* that ably defend various aspects of the sanctuary doctrine from a Biblical perspective.

2 Birthday of Destiny

A New England farmer-turned-preacher, William Miller, was the founder and spark plug of the American Advent Movement. Though Seventh-day Adventists have traveled far beyond Miller's views, he is the grandfather of our sanctuary message, and we have never ceased to stand upon his shoulders. This first of two chapters on the development of our sanctuary doctrine must therefore begin with a look at William Miller.

Though reared in a devoutly Christian home, in early manhood Miller followed the deist philosophies of his friends and became an avowed skeptic. Soon after serving in the War of 1812, however, he found himself hungry for the Saviour's forgiveness and began attending the local Baptist church. One Sunday, in the absence of the pastor, he was asked to read a selection from *Proudfit's Practical Sermons*. During his presentation Miller was so overcome with emotion he was forced to sit down. Many in the congregation wept with him, recognizing the convicting of God's Spirit. Miller eagerly accepted Christ as his substitute and found rest in the merits of His blood.

Immediately after conversion Miller began an intensive study of the Scriptures. His only research tools were *Cruden's Concordance*, the marginal references of his Bible, and some history volumes. While on a methodical march through the Testaments he became fascinated with predictions of Christ's second advent. Certain that the end of the world would come soon, he gave close attention to the time element of these prophecies. In 1818, after two years of study, he was convinced that "the 2300 year-days, extending from 457 B.C. to about A.D. 1843, will bring the climax of prophecy and of human history; and that Jesus will come 'on or before' the Jewish year '1843'" [1]

Startled by his own conclusions, Miller feared that he erred in his research. Four more years he invested in closely examining the Bible. Finally persuaded in 1822 that his discoveries were indeed legitimate, he wrote his statement of belief, "Compendium of Faith." In harmony with his Protestant heritage, this document extolled the assurance of salvation through the death of Jesus. Miller, however, parted paths with contemporary theologians in repeating his radical conclusion reached earlier, that Christ would return "on or before 1843." [2]

A Movement Is Born

During the next nine years, until August of 1831, Miller refrained from publicizing his prophetic discoveries. Gradually, however, the conviction formed that the world needed his message. At first reluctant because of his age, now nearly 50, and his lack of ministerial credentials, he finally consented to his conscience to speak if opportunity knocked. Immediately an invitation arrived to preach in a nearby Baptist church. Upon arriving home from that church the next day, he received another welcome for his prophetic expositions. Soon the doors of hundreds of churches opened to him—Baptist, Congregationalist, Methodist, and others across Northeastern United States and even Eastern Canada. After several years, as the demand for his teaching skyrocketed, Miller entered full-time ministry. By this time he had received a Baptist minister's license, and the next year, 1835, forty-three pastors from various denominations signed a certificate of "Ministerial Recommendation" on his behalf.[3]

As the message of the near Advent spread, a number of ministers left their salaried positions to join Miller's movement. These disciples of the Word provided creative contributions of their own. Josiah Litch, a Methodist clergyman, edited various Millerite publications. Richard Schwarz reports:

"In commenting on Revelation 9 Litch daringly applied the day-year principle of prophetic interpretation to Turkey, predicting its loss of power in August, 1840. This caused considerable discussion and increased interest in Bible prophecy. Thousands, including hundreds of former infidels, interpreted the Ottoman Empire's acceptance of Great Power guarantees on August 11, 1840, as a vindication of Litch's position."[4]

Through the instruction of Litch, a Presbyterian pastor, Charles Fitch, united with the movement. His well-known chart predicting the end of the world in 1843 attracted widespread attention. When this time-setting aroused the ridicule of the Protestant community, Fitch also initiated the proclamation of the second angel's message of Revelation 14, that "Babylon is fallen" [K.J.V.], and the Revelation 18 warning to "come out of her, my people" [K.J.V.].[5] Now thousands left their churches or were disfellowshipped for living the Adventist message.

The Midnight Cry

When the 1843 season set for the end of the world passed without event, Samuel S. Snow concluded from restudying the prophecies that Christ was not to come until the autumn of the following year. At first his views won little following. Most Adventists had refocused their expectation of the end of time upon the coming spring Passover season. But when the spring of 1844 came and went, Snow's teachings offered to the disappointed believers both logical explanation and hope. During mid-August, at the Exeter, New Hampshire, camp meeting, Snow delivered three landmark lectures that won wholehearted approval. Now the specific date of October 22, which he advocated, was adopted and fervently proclaimed. This "Seventh Month Movement" added great impetus to the Adventist awakening, sweeping a host of eager believers away from their churches into the immediate expectation of their Lord.[6]

At this point another minister, George Storrs, added the final plank to the Millerite platform with the use of Christ's parable of the ten virgins. The spring disappointment was interpreted as the tarrying time of the bridegroom. The faithful were urged to watch and be ready, for in a few short weeks Christ would come. Now the rallying cry went forth, "Behold the Bridegroom cometh; go ye out to meet Him!" (see Matt. 25:6). This Midnight Cry electrified the Millerites and brought the movement to its climax.

Everyday life was cast aside. Farmers, ignoring unharvested crops, pleaded with their neighbors to prepare for their Lord's return. Storrs observed: "There is a strong crying with tears, and a consecration of all to God, such as I never witnessed. There is a confidence in this truth such as was never felt in the previous cry, . . . and a weeping or melting glory in it that passes all understanding except to those who have felt it."[7]

The Great Disappointment

By the beginning of October, belongings were sold and the proceeds invested in the spreading of the last warning. Finally the presses stopped rolling, the last goodbyes were exchanged, and the expectant believers waited for the dawn of October 22. The stage was now set for the great Disappointment. In the words of church historian LeRoy Froom:

"All over the land, on that fateful day . . . the Adventist believers had gathered in their homes, in churches or in halls, or wherever they might find refuge from the mockers and the mobs. . . . It was the day of great expectancy and ardent longing. . . . But the sun passed its zenith, and declined toward its setting. The cloud of shining glory for which they strained their eyes, and which they believed would bring their Lord, did not appear. No lightning rent the sky, no earthquake shook the land, no trumpet smote the ear. The westering sun went down silently but relentlessly upon their disappearing hopes. Darkness covered the land, and gloom—irrepressible gloom—settled down upon the waiting, watching host. Grief and despair overwhelmed them all. Men and women wept unashamedly, for their Lord had not come."[8]

Hiram Edson, a heartbroken believer, described their corporate agony:

"Our fondest hopes and expectations were blasted, and such a spirit of weeping came over us as I had never experienced before. It seemed that the loss of all earthly friends could have been no comparison. We wept, and wept, till the day dawn. I mused in my own heart, saying, My advent experience has been the richest and brightest of all my Christian experience. If this had proved a failure, what was the rest of my Christian experience worth? Has the Bible proved a failure? Is there no God, no heaven, no golden home city, no paradise? Is all this but a cunningly devised fable?"[9]

A Remnant Survives and Thrives

Needless to say, the Millerite movement was shattered by the great Disappointment. Most now forsook their former Advent fervor, declaring it to be un-Biblical fanaticism. Some still contended that despite obvious error in interpretation, the movement had been founded by God and was basically sound in Scripture. From this minority, three groups emerged: (1) those who concluded that the 1844 date was incorrect and continued time-setting for the return of Christ, (2) those who maintained faith in Christ's soon advent but resembled traditional Protestantism otherwise, and (3) those who eventually became Seventh-day Adventists.

This latter group seemed doomed to oblivion. Most of them were poor farmers, cut off from the mainstream of Christianity. Not one notable religious leader stood among them. All appearances indicated the early doom of their movement.

How did this little band of believers manage to survive and thrive? And how did their theology gel into a stable doctrinal structure? This is the theme of the chapter that follows.

3 Joy in the Morning

Weeping may last for the night, but a shout of joy comes in the morning" (Ps. 30:5). After that night of bitter tears ending in earnest prayer, Hiram Edson went out to encourage some of the crestfallen believers. Avoiding the road to escape the taunts of neighbors, Edson began trudging across a cornfield. Suddenly he was startled by a revelation that gave birth to the worldwide movement of the Seventh-day Adventist denomination. This chapter will trace the development of Edson's new concept as it grew into the unique understanding that the church has today of the heavenly sanctuary and its judgment.

Here is how Edson described his experience: "While passing through a large field I was stopped about midway of the field. Heaven seemed open to my view, and I saw distinctly and clearly that instead of our High Priest coming out of the Most Holy of the heavenly sanctuary to come to this earth on the tenth day of the seventh month, at the end of the 2300 days, He for the first time entered on that day the second apartment of that sanctuary." [1]

So the solution that erased Edson's perplexity and sparked the birth of the Adventist Church was simple—the Millerites had been correct in their computation of the 2300 years but mistaken about the event to close the prophecy. Rather than ending His work as High Priest, Christ began the second phase of His ministry in the Second Apartment, or Most Holy Place, of the sanctuary. Furthermore, this sanctuary is in heaven; it was not the earth, as Miller had taught.

Immediately Edson began intensive study of this new concept along with O.R.L. Crosier and F. B. Hahn, both fellow former Millerites. Together they concluded that the heavenly sanctuary to be cleansed had been the pattern for the Old Testament sanctuary on earth and that Christ would have to complete the second phase of His ministry in heaven before He could come to bless His waiting people.

Rousing the Scattered Remnant

The trio commissioned Crosier to write out their discoveries, which they jointly published in a paper they called *Day-Dawn* in the autumn of 1845. Ten months later these articles were amplified in the larger *Day-Star* of Cincinnati. Quite a few were impressed with this thorough and systematic explanation of the sanctuary doctrine. Among them were some Sabbathkeeping believers in New England. At a conference of the "scattered remnant" the sanctuary and Sabbath doctrines were inseparably welded together.

During this time a devout young woman, Ellen White, rapidly gained influence through a series of visions she received that endorsed the experience of the Adventist awakening and the emerging sanctuary theology. At each of several historic Bible conferences in 1848 Ellen White had one or two visions that confirmed material others would present from the Bible. Her influence can hardly be overestimated in establishing the Sabbatarian Adventists in their system of beliefs. Yet it must be emphasized that she did not pioneer the discovery of truth. Her role was to endorse and foster faith in that which had been learned through others' Bible study.[2]

Thus 1848 with its Bible conferences was a crucial year in building a doctrinal platform, which included the sanctuary doctrine.[3]

The Shut Door

Meanwhile, the "shut door" theory was adopted by the Sabbathkeeping Adventists. They believed that when Jesus began His final ministry on October 22, 1844, His intercession for sinners ceased, and the door of probation was shut to those who had not accepted the Millerite message. They insisted that there was no hope of salvation for those who did not believe before the Disappointment.

Until 1850 at least, Adventism's two principal points of "present truth" were the Sabbath and the shut door.[4] In time, however, it became obvious that souls were being won and thus probation must still be open.

For a while Ellen herself misunderstood the matter of probation's shut door. According to the Ellen G. White Estate (the official denominational trustees of her writings), she "misinterpreted"[5] her December, 1844, vision to teach this mistaken concept. It is further reported that "in the five years from December, 1844, to January, 1850, Ellen White had gained a much clearer and broader understanding of the phrase 'and the door was shut' [K.J.V.] in Matthew 25—admittedly, a fundamental change."[6]

Investigating the Judgment

During the 1850s the shut door was gradually and quietly abandoned and replaced by the investigative judgment. As the pioneers understood this new doctrine, the sins of believers, when specifically confessed, are transferred through the blood of Christ to the books of the sanctuary in heaven. In 1844 Christ "shut the door" of the first apartment of the sanctuary to enter the Most Holy Place. Then began a work of scrutinizing the characters of His saints. Those whose lives measured up to God's law had their sins blotted out, or cleansed from the sanctuary. Those who somehow failed to reflect the image of Jesus fully had their names blotted out of the book of life. Falling short of perfection, they could not be sealed, and their sins remained on record to seal their doom. When this work of investigative judgment finally would be complete, Christ could cease His mediation as High Priest and return to this earth to reward its inhabitants according to their works.[7]

The roots of this new concept of judgment go back as far as 1842 and the Millerite Josiah Litch. Others contributed various features as the doctrine took shape.[8] Interestingly, not until 1857 did James White throw his full support behind the pre-Advent scrutiny of the saints. He then coined the term *investigative judgment.*

This doctrine has often been challenged through the years from both without and within the church. Most notable of numerous dissenters within Adventist ranks were O.R.L. Crosier himself (creator turned critic before the actual formation of the Seventh-day Adventist organization), John H. Kellogg, Albion Ballenger, Dudley M. Canright, and more recently, Robert D. Brinsmead. The latest challenge brought by Desmond Ford has raised quite a furor and has posed a real threat to the church's historic interpretations. Although Ford no longer holds an Adventist teaching position and ministerial credentials, his questions remain to haunt many loyal Adventists. I understand that more than one hundred Adventist ministers and teachers have left denominational service, either voluntarily or by termination, in recent times. The cause of this disheartening disaster was their rejection of the investigative judgment and the related issue of Ellen White's doctrinal authority. One of them, Walter Rea, accuses the church of "having devised one of the most elaborate systems of salvation by works that the world has ever seen since the fall of Jerusalem in A.D. 70."[9] This is quite a charge! Is it true?

Students of denominational history generally acknowledge that the founders of the sanctuary doctrine struggled with legalism. Exhibit A would be the total omission of any reference to salvation through Christ's sacrifice in the list of "Leading Doctrines as taught by the Review."[10] Ellen White lamented that the 1888 Minneapolis Conference was the first time she had heard clear teaching about salvation (except in private conversations with her husband),[11] and this after forty-five years in the Advent Movement. This explains the initial resistance by many church leaders to the gospel during that conference.

Considering their pre-1888 background, we should expect to see immature and even legalistic elements in the pioneers' proclamation of the judgment and the sanctuary. Can we today cherish each pillar of their genuine Biblical foundation and yet mature in our own understanding of their glorious truths?

Reflections of the First Century

Such a rescue of truth amid error had been accomplished before, in the birth of Christianity itself. The New Testament records the great disappointment of the disciples when the death of Christ fulfilled the time prophecy of Daniel 9. They made the same mistake the Millerites later repeated with another prophecy in Daniel—totally misunderstanding the events that climaxed the time prediction. Yet despite their dismal error, they still comprised God's movement of destiny, and He did not forsake them.

Amid the scorn of unbelievers the disciples bitterly mourned, " 'But we were hoping that it was He who was going to redeem Israel' " (Luke 24:21). Just as Edson was given light centuries later while trudging along in despair, so the obscure Cleopas had received light on the road to Emmaus. Despite this revelation, the disciples were yet immature in their understanding of doctrine forty days after the resurrection. They wondered, " 'Lord, is it at this time You are restoring the kingdom to Israel?' " (Acts 1:6). Even then they expected a temporal reign for Jesus, obviously ignorant of His upcoming ministry in the heavenly sanctuary. What is more, the apostles believed in a shut door for outsiders to their Jewish heritage. Then Peter received a vision that the Gentiles were to be evangelized, which he initially did not understand (see chap. 10:17).

To round out this remarkable and undeniable parallel, we note that the tiny and despised band of disciples expanded into a worldwide movement, ever to live and learn, grow and share. Since every Christian of whatever denomination participates in this history of a great disappointment, shut door, and continuing struggle with legalism, the enemies of Adventism would do well to remember their own heritage before they presume to mock.

Now, having reviewed the history of God's leadership in the Adventist experience, let us examine that unique pillar of truth, the sanctuary, in its various aspects. We may begin by investigating the meaning of judgment.

4 The Solution for "Sadventism"

Adventism today may be subdivided into several tribes. First, we have "Gladventists," or happy Adventist Christians. Thank God for them! Unfortunately, we also find "Badventists"—hypocrites and prodigals. When a Sabbath sermon transgresses the stroke of noon, "Madventists" stalk out in disgust. At the end of the rope are "Sadventists." Nothing is more pitiful than a sad Adventist—one who sincerely repents and tries to live in faith but does not enjoy the peace that is supposed to accompany commitment.

In recent years many guilt-ridden Sadventists have broken the bonds of legalism to rejoice in gospel freedom. Cherishing the blessed assurance of God's favor as manifest in Christ's sacrifice, some of these have thought it necessary to discard the landmark Adventist doctrine of the sanctuary to avoid the scrutiny of the investigative judgment. They even denounce this uniquely Adventist doctrine as face-saving fiction invented to excuse the great Disappointment and, worse yet, a device of the devil to hijack confidence in Christ.

Crucial Questions

"Why," they demand, "should those already 'accepted in the beloved' [Eph. 1:6, K.J.V.] be now subjected to the scrutiny of judgment? Didn't Jesus clearly state that ' "he who hears My word, and believes Him who sent Me, has eternal life, and does not come into judgment" ' [John 5:24]?"

"No!" disagrees a loyal Adventist. "My King James Bible teaches that believers are judged. We escape 'condemnation,' but there is still a judgment all must face."

Then those who reject the investigative judgment will report that the King James Version is inconsistent here. In John 5:22 the Greek noun *krisis* is correctly translated "judgment," but two verses later the same word in the same context is changed to "condemnation." Even that New Testament pillar passage in Revelation 14 employs *krisis* to proclaim that 'the hour of his judgment is come' [K.J.V.]. Not the hour of His condemnation, but of His judgment, a judgment that, according to the words of Jesus, does not involve believers. Walter Martin, a writer who has made his mark dealing with cults, charges that "in John 5:24 the Greek deals a devastating blow to the Seventh-day Adventist concept of investigative judgment." [1] Dare we ignore this challenge?

Those who defy Adventist doctrine press their point with another perplexing passage: " ' "He who believes in Him is *not* judged" ' [John 3:18]. This only makes sense," they assert. [2] "Why must God spend more than a hundred years investigating records when already ' "the Lord knows those who are His" ' [2 Tim. 2:19]?"

These questions bring considerable consternation to some Adventists. Rarely are the problems squarely faced. Usually Adventists escape the attack of these troublesome texts by finding refuge in those safe and familiar passages that bind the movement together, such as James 2:12: "So speak and so act, as those who are to be judged by the law of liberty."

"The work of Christ," we contend, "does not release us from accountability. We are told to ' "give an account of your stewardship" ' [Luke 16:2]. Wherever there is accountability, there is judgment. Paul warns that 'we must all appear before the judgment seat of Christ' [2 Cor. 5:10]. Surely these scriptures all show that Christians must face judgment."

"Wait a minute!" Another challenge intrudes. "You can't quote Paul to prove your investigative judgment. He tells us Christ is the judge. You teach that He's your defense attorney. How can Jesus both judge believers and represent them at the same time? You can't have it both ways."

Oh, well. Back to Revelation 14. There it clearly states that during earth's final gospel proclamation " 'the hour of His judgment *has* come.' " [3]

And so it goes. Both traditional and "evangelical" [4] Adventists hide behind the fortress of their favorite texts, trying to avoid the other group's bombardment of Biblical proofs. Each side cites convincing support in Scripture. Many honest seekers of truth, filled with confusion and despair, wonder what to do.

Searching for Solutions

"Don't chase the devil's dogs," many advise. "We have the truth. Ellen White said it, I believe it, and that settles it for me! The stubborn will drown in their doubts, but we have a message to preach. We don't have time to waste. Let's get on with our mission!"

But others who are just as committed to the message and mission of this church voice concern with such a strategy: "This is no trifling annoyance to be brushed aside. We have a fundamental challenge here, an iceberg that must be met. What right do we have to baptize a thousand a day if we cannot defend our message from the Bible?" While some who don't have time to waste on doubts are wasting their evenings watching Monday night football and other "innocent" diversions, others are earnestly searching the Scriptures, studying to show themselves approved unto God and to give answers to those who want a reason for their Adventist hope.

These answers must come from the Bible. Ellen White herself, faithful prophet of God for this movement, emphatically placed her writings beneath the greater light of God's Word and insisted that the Bible, not her books, be the standard of doctrine. Referring to her ministry, she admonished that "the Spirit was not given—nor can it ever be bestowed—to supersede the Bible; for the Scriptures explicitly state that the word of God is the standard by which all teaching and experience must be tested."[5]

Discovery in a Jewish Courtroom

Thank God, there are convincing scriptural answers for all who have ears to hear. The key to solving this doctrinal dilemma is in the method and meaning of Biblical judgment. The Hebrew legal system differed drastically from modern America's. To begin with, *The Jewish Encyclopedia* informs us that "attorneys at law are unknown in Jewish law."[6] Witnesses of the crime pressed charges. And who was there to defend the accused? The judge. "In criminal cases the law imposed upon the judges the duty of carefully guarding the prisoner's rights."[7] "Judges leaned always to the side of the defendant and gave him the advantage of every possible doubt."[8] Only when overwhelmed by evidence would the judge reluctantly abandon his defense of the accused and pronounce a verdict of guilt.

The judge, then, was more than a neutral and impartial guardian of justice. He was on the side of the accused, biased in favor of acquittal.[9]

Now we may see how Jesus, our judge, can also serve as our defender. There is no conflict in this dual role—it is in fact necessary for Jesus to defend us as our judge.

In certain situations the Hebrew system made exception and permitted an advocate to plead for the accused. *The Jewish Encyclopedia* tells us that the husband could represent his wife in cases that involved his own rights.[10] Christ, the bridegroom of the church, purchased us with His precious blood. How fitting that He now defends that investment, in our union with Him, as our intercessor.

Here we see why it was legally necessary for Jesus to share our nature, to be "the man Christ Jesus," before He could minister as the "mediator between God and men" (1 Tim. 2:5, K.J.V.). Because He joined the human family, He has the right to protect our mutual interests by interceding as our High Priest in heaven's court.

Another touching evidence of God's love for His children is shown by a further provision of the Hebrew legal system: "In the nature of things some parties cannot plead for themselves. Infants, boys under thirteen or girls under twelve, the deaf and dumb, and lunatics can plead only through a guardian; and it is the duty of the court to appoint a guardian for such, if they have none."[11]

We are helpless, like sheep, and cannot plead for ourselves. Unable even to understand our needs, we are unfit to deal with the devil. So our loving Father in heaven has appointed a sympathetic High Priest to intercede for His children against the cruel charges of our accuser. What a wonderful Friend.

Judgment Is a Favor!

No wonder that David and Solomon both longed to be sentenced by God's judgment (see Ps. 43:1; 35:24; 26:1; 1 Kings 8:32). Throughout the Old Testament God's children found joy in His judgment. "A father of the fatherless and a judge for the widows, is God in His holy habitation" (Ps. 68:5).

The vivid scene of Zechariah 3 demonstrates dramatically that God is on our side when we are judged. The devil presents his case against us. *(Satan,* according to the margin of Zechariah 3:1, means "accuser" or "adversary.") He has witnessed the success of his temptations and now presses charges against Joshua, who as high priest represents God's people. *(Joshua* is Hebrew for "Jesus," which means "Saviour," as shown by Matthew 1:21.) He bears the "filthy garments" (Zech. 3:3) of the sinners he represents. God, in His role as defender/judge, rules in favor of His family:

"And the Lord said to Satan, 'The Lord rebuke you, Satan! Indeed, the Lord who has chosen Jerusalem rebuke you! Is this not a brand plucked from the fire?' . . . And he spoke and said to those who were standing before him saying, 'Remove the filthy garments from him.' Again he said to him, 'See, I have taken your iniquity away from you and will clothe you with festal robes.' Then I said, 'Let them put a clean turban on his head.' So they put a clean turban on his head and clothed him with garments, while the angel of the Lord was standing by" (verses 2-5).

God does not argue with the devil—His people are unclean. But by the blood of His Son we conquer in the judgment. Satan's charges are dismissed, and heaven celebrates:

" 'Now the salvation, and the power, and the kingdom of our God and the authority of His Christ have come, for the accuser of our brethren has been thrown down, who accuses them before our God day and night. And they overcame him because of the blood of the Lamb and because of the word of their testimony, and they did not love their life even to death' " (Rev. 12:10, 11).

The judgment is good news because of the blood of Christ. Satan disputes our right to rest in Jesus, accusing us of unfaithfulness and unfitness for heaven. By rejecting and persecuting God's people, this world concurs with the devil's charges. Under attack from every side, we long for God to deliver us and vindicate our relationship with Him. We therefore welcome judgment.

In spite of our confessed sinfulness, we need not feel frightened by God's judgment. He is predisposed in favor of our vindication, and all the evidence He needs is in the cross to which we cling. This judgment vindicates our names in the Lamb's book of life. God does not question our relationship with Him; He defends and ratifies it. He does not initiate a favorable standing with us, but displays and endorses the security in Christ we have enjoyed since we accepted Him. In summary, judgment is a favor, not a threat, to the Christian.

What refreshing, revitalizing power this concept of judgment has for Gladventism! Although our pioneers may have overlooked the full gospel perspective of the pre-Advent judgment, it is genuine Biblical truth that "evangelical" Adventists should eagerly cherish.

Another Judgment Long Ago

In God's work of vindicating us, certain facts are predetermined, fixed in a previous judgment at Calvary: " 'Now judgment is upon this world; now the ruler of this world shall be cast out' " (John 12:31). At that time this sinful world and all its citizens received the just verdict of death. The sentence was executed upon us through the punishment received by our Substitute. But the same cross that decreed our guilt likewise established our righteousness in Christ. The resurrection placed beyond question the validity of that redemption (see Rom. 4:25).

We Must Live in Faith

The glorious reality that Christ conquered Satan and the world on the cross does not release us from accountability today. We are under obligation to accept that reconciliation now and will be judged according to our attitude to His act of redemption. All depends upon whether we choose to live a life of faith in Jesus. Saving faith values His sacrifice above everything this world offers—even life itself. For us, then, the judgment is concerned with whether or not we yield ourselves to live this kind of faith.

Here is a personal experience to illustrate the purpose of judgment for Christians. Recently I rode the Amtrak rails from Los Angeles to San Diego. As the train skirted the beautiful Pacific coastline, the conductor began his judgment of who was worthy to ride his train. Because I held a ticket I felt no threat to secure passage. It was predetermined that my worthiness was based exclusively on that ticket. Thus the investigation was not of my achievements or failures, but of my claim to hold the ticket. The inspection did not threaten my security, but manifested it.

Likewise with us before God. We must all give account of what we did with our Ticket, Jesus. Our personal worthiness, which was condemned at Calvary, does not come under investigation.[12] Only our claim to have lived by faith in Jesus is evaluated. If we have chosen to receive Him, we need not fear the judgment. But if we have rejected Him through rebellion or neglect, we are already condemned. This world is considered sinful, Jesus taught, " 'because they do not believe in Me' " (John 16:9).

Passengers who have purchased tickets must not discard them before they have reached their destination. They must continue to hold them, or they have no claim to the ride. Similarly, it is possible for us to rebel and leave Jesus; there is no such thing as once saved, always saved. Our initial acceptance of Him does not guarantee that we want His life today. Our faith in Christ must be maintained in daily living.

Faith Means Obedience

When we believe in Jesus, that choice is reflected in our lifestyle. Our pursuits are not those of the flesh, but in the joy of forgiveness we seek to please our

Redeemer. Jesus is now the king of our lives. Our works are by no means perfect, but they do testify of the influence of the Saviour and thus serve as evidence of a decision. Although this judgment does not involve our success in sanctification, it is concerned with whether or not we repent in forsaking the world to believe in Jesus and keep His commandments. Faith in Christ works by love (Gal. 5:6). "Love . . . is the fulfillment of the law" (Rom. 13:10). *Therefore, a life of faith in Jesus will honor God's holy law of ten commandments.* (See Rom. 3:31; Rev. 14:12; James 2:10-12.)

Whatever happened to good old-fashioned repentance? "Born-again" Christians paste Jesus stickers on their radar detectors and speed through life in defiance of law, claiming God as their "copilot." Even the Adventist Church is infected by this cheap "faith." We need bold souls in the pulpit who will cry out like the prophet Nathan, "Thou art the man!" And we must have humble and contrite Davids to confess, "I have sinned." (See 2 Samuel 12:7, 13.)

Those few ministers who dare to rebuke television abuse, for example, are regarded as narrow-minded. "Please, pastor, don't be so prudish. The only reason I own a TV is to watch the late-night nudes—I-I mean the late-night news!"

Televised immorality is a deadly snake that has bitten many members. Yet it is not the primary poisoner of Adventists. We take pride in the clean television programs we watch, forgetting that the basic nature of sin is simply to live outside of Christ. Hollywood's biggest lie is that we can find fulfillment in a clean and caring lifestyle without fellowship with God. Wholesome worldliness, more often than the heat of porno passion, divorces lukewarm members from their Lord. Sportscasts can outscore the Saviour in the competition for our commitment. And it may shock us to learn that "innocent" family shows, in modeling morality without reference to God, probably do more than anything else to secularize our lives and ruin our dependence upon grace.

Is this hard to believe? Take inventory: Do your favorite programs show families having daily worship together? Do your TV role models take time for personal devotions? Do they encourage one another with Bible promises? People are cute, popular, smart, successful, and even loving while ignoring God in daily life. The influence of this godless, artificial morality may affect us more than we realize. What are your everyday values? Do *you* have daily family worship? When was the last time you enjoyed a non-Sabbath evening—or even a Sabbath evening—reading God's Word? Do you visit the poor and the sick? "No time"? Why are we so tied up? Maybe we would find freedom to live for God if we would divorce our television. Rather than staying up late watching the bad news, we could be getting up early for the Good News. Perhaps we have a Christian experience that is "for the birds" because we do not rise with the birds to praise God for the dawning day and welcome His fellowship.

Every honest Adventist, it seems, would have to conclude that television has become a channel of hell. Of course, there is nothing wrong with the tube itself—thousands have found Christ through this medium. Students of the Bible can track fulfillment of prophecies with the news. Some Christians actually control the unruly appliance. We cannot judge one another—we each give account for ourselves to God for our choice of values.

Television is not our only refuge from God's grace. It is becoming more fashionable to chain a polished gold cross around our necks than to carry the rugged old cross with its splinters. Faithful preachers who suggest that the adorning of our bodies should be replaced by helping the poor or by reversing the shameful decline in mission offerings are called legalists. In view of the worldliness and lukewarm condition of our churches, well may we wonder Where is that heartbroken repulsion of sin that always accompanies true faith?

Here is the point of all this: *The faith that covers us with Christ is a life-changing principle that expells worldliness.* It is not an *excuse* but an *exchange.* We exchange our guilt for His pardon, our weakness for His strength, our ignorance for His wisdom, and our secular lifestyle for a life with Him, a life of trusting obedience to His will as expressed in His law.

How sad that many "faithful" Adventists will perish, not for evil habits, but for living a wholesome life of building and planting, eating and drinking, marrying and giving in marriage—without a daily walk with Jesus. Therefore our crucial concern in the judgment is whether our faith regards the sacrifice of Christ more than the good and bad things of this world. This faith will follow Jesus anywhere He leads.

Legalism?

Is this obedience legalism? Only if done in appeasement—that is, to win or maintain God's favor. But when our hearts are charged with love for Him who first loved us and we in *appreciation for forgiveness* follow Him fully, seeking to please Him in everything, we are not legalists. The church desperately needs to see Christian standards, such as diet and dress, in the light of the gospel.

Whoever truly follows Jesus needs not maintain a scrapbook of progress in the Christian life. And we completely forget about keeping score. Confident of salvation, we are freed from anxiety about our faults—set free to live unto God and our neighbors. This is a lifestyle that honors God's holy law. But our hope is not in attaining an immaculate record, since our personal righteousness was already judged and condemned on the cross. The investigative judgment today scrutinizes the sincerity of our claim to trust in Jesus.

From the unlikely world of baseball comes an illustration to help us understand the judgment. As our substitute, Jesus pinch-hit a home run. He has provided the game-winning hit for everyone. But our run will not score unless we circle the base paths with Him—He will hold our hand. We are born into the devil's dugout, and there is plenty to keep us preoccupied. God must first get our attention to inform us of the score against us and our inability to work our way back into the ball game. Next He proclaims the wonderful work of Jesus. Having acquainted us with these saving facts, He then seeks to persuade us that what He offers is worth more than the toys in the dugout. We are urged to repent of our foolishness, forsake the devil, and circle the "straight and narrow" base paths with Jesus. But we must stay out of the batter's box—there is no need for us to manufacture a batting average. For us to swing a bat would be to deny Jesus. Having already struck out for eternity, we cannot now compete with Christ's accomplishments for us. Our obedience to God must be in celebration of His salvation.

So the crucial questions in the judgment regarding our salvation are these: Do we consider the gift of Jesus to be more valuable than the devil's pleasures and counterfeit fulfillments? Do we trust Christ's substitution and refrain from competing with His accomplishments? Are we willing to accept a straight and narrow pathway for the privilege of life with Jesus? There is no reference whatever to our batting average.

"Why, God?"

Now we must face the question Why would such a judgment be necessary, since God knows who His children are? Obviously this investigation is not to inform the Lord. Thus it must be to enlighten His creation.

The great controversy between good and evil began before the earth existed. *The issues concerning our forgiveness focus upon the integrity of the Forgiver Himself and involve the unfallen universe.* God's character and quality of government were questioned and challenged by Lucifer, prince of angels. Through selfish ambition he aspired to gain control of the throne of heaven (see Isa. 14:12-14). Jesus called him " 'the father of lies' " (John 8:44), and his deceptions captured the hearts of a third of the angels (see Rev. 12:4). Although most of the angels refused to be moved by Lucifer's lies, doubts can linger and harass even the most loyal and obedient.

The devil claimed he still belonged in heaven's councils after being cast out (see Job 1:6, 7). Was it fair to exclude him while sinners were forgiven on earth? God has shown Himself anxious to defend His Fatherhood before the heavenly host against Satan's lies (see chap. 2:1-6).

The cross was "to demonstrate His righteousness, because in the forbearance of God He passed over the sins previously committed" (Rom. 3:25). Although God did then vindicate His fairness in forgiveness—that He can "be just and the justifier of the one who has faith in Jesus" (verse 26)—misgivings still remain. Why are some who claim Christ accepted and others rejected, since "we all stumble in many ways" (James 3:2)? Is it true that " 'God is not one to show partiality' " (Acts 10:34)? Then why did He choose the Jews " 'to be a people for His own possession out of all the peoples who are on the face of the earth' " (Deut. 7:6)? If God is so good, then how come "those who were His own did not receive Him" (John 1:11)? Does everyone have equal opportunity? Is it fair for God to punish "all ungodliness and unrighteousness of men" (Rom. 1:18)? Can He prove that sufficient information about Himself "is evident within them; for God made it evident to them" (verse 19)? If He is love, then why does He allow innocent babies to die? Why do elderly saints suffer endless months with cancer? Even humans would not treat loved ones like that. Are they nicer than God in some ways?

Have you ever wondered, "Why, God?" Our questions are *not* entirely quenched by Calvary. The cross did prove beyond question that God can be supremely loving, but many vital questions still survive. The bottom line is this: Has the love demonstrated at the cross been consistently offered to everyone alike throughout history?

God Himself on Trial

The evidence of God's goodness to the human race is important to celestial beings.[13] Since His kingdom of love operates through the confiding affection and trusting loyalty of His universe, it is essential that He settle these questions. Romans 3:3-7 reveals that God will condescend to allow His activities to be audited. Paul exclaimed, "Let God be found true, though every man be found a liar, as it is written, 'That Thou mightest be justified in Thy words, and mightest prevail when thou art judged'" (verse 4).

In summary, it is clear that there is a judgment that will involve three themes:

1. The vindication of God in His dealings with sin and sinners since the rebellion of Lucifer in heaven, thus reaffirming His right to rule the universe by His holy law of love.

2. As a by-product of the vindication of God, the defeat of Satan's challenge and the concomitant damnation of those who share Satan's mistrust and disobedience.

3. The vindication of those who live by faith in Jesus—the overcoming of the charges raised by their accusers and the endorsing of the security they have enjoyed since accepting Christ.

The Judge Is on Our Side!

Those who have left the Adventist Church reject a pre-Advent judgment as legalistic and un-Biblical. How unfortunate! How unfair!

The judgment is God's showcase to vindicate before an onlooking universe the freedom He grants to those who live in Jesus. (The chapters that follow in this book should clarify this further.)

But this judgment is more than merely sound theology. In this doctrine Jesus comforts Sadventists: "'Do not be afraid, little flock, for your Father has chosen gladly to give you the kingdom'" (Luke 12:32).

The Judge is on our side! This is our message for a lonely, frightened world.

5 The Rise and Fall of Antichrist

E ver since *The Late Great Planet Earth* was raptured into the heights of the best-seller list, the American imagination has had a fearful fascination for books about the antichrist. Even supermarkets and drugstores sport a variety of religious fiction thrillers, many of them spiced with novel speculation about the magic and mysterious number 666. As book after book is embarrassed into oblivion by aborted predictions, new ones are born, each destined to similar self-destruction. Meanwhile we wait for their overdue antichrist.

Amid these falling leaves there stands one evergreen. *The Great Controversy*, authored by Ellen White, is more relevant today than it was a century ago. (Have you read it recently?) What is its secret of long life? Truth. Shunning speculation, this book stands upon the foundation laid by the pioneers of Protestantism—men whose names are memorialized by denominations that have forgotten their prophetic heritage.

Luther and his fellow Reformers had no doubts about the identity of antichrist. They pointed fearless fingers toward Rome. Were they correct? Could it be possible that all the time contemporary Protestants have been scouting the horizon for the antichrist, it has been basking in their own backyard?

Let us examine the prophetic faith of the fathers of Protestantism. Why have their children forsaken them? And how does the doctrine of a pre-Advent judgment climax their discoveries? So far in this book we have seen that the judgment is good news and makes good sense as well. Now we must locate its place in the parade of prophetic fulfillments.

The timing of this judgment is anchored in Daniel 7. Verse 10 reports that "'the court sat, and the books were opened.'" When and where does this judgment take place? Who is involved? What is the verdict and its execution?

The key to understanding the time frame of this judgment is the "little horn" (verse 8, K.J.V.), the Old Testament counterpart of the "beast" of Revelation 13. Both are symbols of the Antichrist. Daniel 7 predicted that this evil power would ravage the saints before God finally interrupts its operation. Upon identifying this little horn and learning its time of operation, we should be able to answer our questions.

Who Is the Antichrist?

According to H. G. Guinness—who was not a Seventh-day Adventist:

"The main points in the nature, character, and actings of this 'little horn' [K.J.V.], which we must note in order to discover the power intended, are these:

"1. Its *place:* within the body of the fourth empire.

"2. The *period* of its origin: soon after the division of the Roman territory into ten kingdoms.

"3. Its *nature: different* from the other kingdoms, though in some respects like them. It was a horn, but with eyes and mouth. It would be a kingdom like the rest, a monarchy; but its kings would be overseers or bishops and prophets.

"4. Its *moral character:* boastful and blasphemous; great words spoken against the Most High.

"5. Its *lawlessness:* it would claim authority over times and laws.

"6. Its *opposition to the saints:* it would be a *persecuting* power, and that for so long a period that it would wear out the saints of the Most High, who would be given into its hand for a time.

"7. Its *duration:* 'time, [two] times, and an half [a time]' [K.J.V.], or 1260 years.

"8. Its *doom:* it would suffer the loss of its *dominion* before it was itself destroyed. 'They shall take away his dominion, to consume and to destroy it unto the end' [K.J.V.]." [1]

Three main explanations of this little horn are advanced by commentators from three different schools of interpretations: [2]

1. **Preterist** [3]—that it represents Antiochus Epiphanes, a Seleucid king of the Greek Empire who desecrated the Jewish Temple in the second century B.C.

2. **Futurist**—that it represents a future fulfillment in a final antichrist.

3. **Historicist**—that it represents the historical Roman Catholic Church.

Interestingly, both the preterist and futurist methods of interpretation are rooted in the Catholic Counter-Reformation of the latter part of the sixteenth century. They were designed to destroy the historicist teaching of Protestantism. [4] Let us examine each of these interpretations.

King Antiochus Eliminated

In this twentieth century the preterest position has been popular. The fulfillment of the arrogant little horn is "most frequently attributed to Antiochus Epiphanes." [5]

At first glance Antiochus appears quite plausible. He did blasphemously style himself Theos Epiphanes, which means "the manifestation of God." [6] He also changed the laws of worship and ruthlessly persecuted God's chosen people. However, this Antiochus assumption is seriously challenged by the following facts:

1. The little horn arises after the fourth world power of Daniel 7, which is Rome, not the third kingdom, Greece. Antiochus, as we noted previously, was a

Greek king and thus is disqualified.[7]

Antiochus did not rise after ten kings. He was only eighth in the Seleucid line.[8] *The Pulpit Commentary* contends that "there is nothing said to indicate that the kings are successive, but the inference rather is that they are contemporaries. The attempts are many that have been made to make out ten kings before Epiphanes, but they have all failed."[9]

3. Antiochus was not different from his predecessors, nor was he "larger in appearance than . . . [his] associates" (Dan. 7:20). Indeed, his father, not he, was known as Antiochus the Great.

4. The activities of Antiochus fail to fulfill the time demands of the prophecy. "The most nearly contemporary account, in Maccabees 1:54-59; 4:52-54, is overwhelmingly precise in stating that he interrupted the temple services for *three years and ten days* (from Chislev 15, 168, to Chislev 25, 165)."[10]

5. The demise of Antiochus also missed the mark of prophecy, since the kingdom following Greece was Rome, not the everlasting kingdom of the saints foretold by Daniel 7:27. Furthermore, the little horn was to be " ' "annihilated and destroyed *to the end*" ' " (verse 26, margin). None could argue that the downfall of Antiochus nearly two centuries before Christ was the end of the world.

6. Another argument against identifying the little horn as Antiochus is the unlikelihood that the heavenly court would need to assemble on such a grand scale just to judge one king.[11]

In the light of this evidence from history, the idea that Antiochus Epiphanes might be the little horn of Daniel 7 is indefensible.

Futurists, unlike the preterists, correctly acknowlege the end-of-time destruction of the little horn. However, they err in limiting the activities of the little horn to the last days. They also overlook what happened in history to fulfill the prediction of four world kingdoms followed by the division of the fourth empire. With these two basic flaws the futurists quickly disqualify themselves from further consideration here.

Papal Rome the Antichrist

Of the proposed explanations of the little horn only one remains—the historicist indictment of the papacy. Although Seventh-day Adventists have long taken their stand on this point, it must be remembered that centuries earlier the Protestant Reformation established this interpretation. Martin Luther and John Knox both risked their lives in proclaiming this position.[12] King James I of England, who ordered the translation of the famous Authorized Version of the Bible, also concluded that the little horn is the papacy.[13] So did the eminent mathematician, philosopher, and Bible student Sir Isaac Newton.[14] Even America's first prophetic expositor, the Puritan John Cotton, three centuries ago identified the papacy as being represented by Daniel's little horn.[15]

In our age of ecumenical goodwill it is fashionable to dismiss the overwhelming testimony of past centuries as so much bold rhetoric from overzealous and immature reformers. To do this is to overlook the painstaking scholarship that led these men of God to acknowledge reluctantly such unpopular and life-threatening truth.

H. G. Guinness, after providing the eight-point analysis of the little horn we referred to previously, concludes: "Here are eight distinct and perfectly tangible features. If they all meet in one great reality, if we find them all characterizing one and the same power, can we question that *that* is the power intended? They do all meet in the Roman Papacy, . . . and we are therefore bold to say *it is the great and evil reality predicted.*" [16]

A brief survey of the facts endorses this position. The Roman Catholic Church certainly came out of Rome, emerging as a dominant power after the fall and division of the Roman Empire. Because of its religious nature, it was " ' "different from the previous ones" ' " (Dan. 7:24), which were merely political kingdoms that had defeated the Roman government. Its unwarranted assumption of divine titles, plus the perversion of the gospel truth in the sanctuary, easily qualify as blasphemy.

With the other particulars of this prophecy finding striking fulfillment in the history of the Catholic Church, we may now ask, What about the 1260 days? We will save the discussion of the day-year principle for a later chapter, and first review the parade of scholars who have interpreted these 1260 days of Daniel 7 as representing 1260 actual years.

As far back as the late twelfth century, the Catholic scholar Joachim of Floris, who was summoned by church leaders in 1192 to answer charges of heresy, applied the day-year principle to the 1260 days. [17] Even so, Joachim was preceded by some three centuries by several Jewish scholars who applied the day-year principle to Daniel's prophecies. Besides several Reformation theologians who understood the 1260 days to be fulfilled in actual years of papal supremacy were King James I of England, Sir Isaac Newton, and a host of prophetic expositors in the early nineteenth century. [18] All this before the existence of the Seventh-day Adventist Church!

Desmond Ford, in his 1978 commentary on Daniel, reported that "expositors vary in the way they have applied this period, but most have done so in such a manner as to span the centuries from about the time of Justinian, when the pope was declared head over all the churches and corrector of heretics, till the age of Napoleon, when the Papacy lost its temporal power. It was exactly 1260 years after the memorable decree of Justinian (A.D. 533) that another decree, this time from Napoleon's government, was promulgated, aiming at reducing papal influence in Europe. Five years after the decree of Justinian, the third of the Arian powers opposing papal supremacy received its deathblow. Similarly, five years after the French decree, Berthier of France invaded the Vatican and suspended for a time the papal government, imprisoning the pope." [19]

We may safely conclude that the Roman Catholic Church, not Antiochus Epiphanes or some yet-to-be-revealed villain, completely meets the demands of this prophecy and is indeed the little horn—the Antichrist.

Time of the Judgment

Having identified the little horn, we may seek to know the time of the judgment. Some suggest that this judgment must have happened in the first century because at His ascension Christ proclaimed that " 'all authority has been given to Me in heaven and on earth' " (Matt. 28:18). For the following reasons, this cannot be so:

1. In spite of the victory of the cross Satan is still called "the god of this world" (2 Cor. 4:4). The total effects of Calvary's accomplishments will not be realized " 'until the period of restoration of all things about which God spoke by the mouth of His holy prophets from ancient time' " (Acts 3:21). Right now "the whole world lies in the power of the evil one" (1 John 5:19). No such disgrace will remain after the eternal and omnipotent kingdom is set up at Christ's coming.

2. There is a tightly woven chronological sequence in Daniel 7 that Edward Heppenstall noted: "Daniel the prophet sees in vision a series of events, one following the other. 'As I was continually gazing' is the expression used nine times to show the sequence of the respective scenes appearing before him in continuous and successive action. . . . If each empire was to follow the one previously mentioned, then the judgment of verses 9, 10, 22, 26 must also follow the period of the apostate horn's supremacy of verses 8, 21, 25.[20]

The judgment occurs *after* the reign of the little horn and *before* its final destruction (please refer to chart on the following page, and notice Daniel 7:24-27). Since the little horn did not even exist until after the fifth-century breakup of the Roman Empire, the concept of a first-century fulfillment must be disqualified.

In fact, this judgment must begin in our modern era, since it happens after the three and one-half times, or 1260 years, of papal rule (refer to chart once more and to verses 25, 26). Thus it must start sometime following 1798. And it must end before the coming of Christ, when the saints receive the kingdom—since their possession of the kingdom is a result of his judgment's verdict (see verses 22, 27).

So the general time frame of the judgment is evident—it commences sometime after 1798 and concludes before the return of Jesus. We will learn the specific year to begin this judgment as we study the prophecies of Daniel 8 and 9 in the next four chapters of this book.

Verdict of the Judgment

Only two questions remain to be answered here: Who are involved in the judgment? and What is the verdict and its execution? Answers will be apparent as we mark how each of the three elements of the judgment already noted in chapter four is also present here in Daniel 7:

1. *God's rulership is vindicated* in the face of the devil's challenge. Before the celestial court Christ is " 'given dominion, glory and a kingdom, that all the

DANIEL 7

	VISION (VERSES 3-14)	INTERPRETATION		
		SUMMARY STATEMENT (VERSES 17, 18)	GENERAL OUTLINE (VERSES 19-22)	SPECIFIC OUTLINE (VERSES 23-27)
GOD CHALLENGED	4 beasts: First = lion; Second = bear; Another = leopard; Fourth = dreadful beast has 10 horns; Little horn (LH) uproots 3 horns boasts	4 beasts = 4 kings arising	LH comes up, overpowers saints	4th beast = 4th kingdom; 10 horns = 10 kings; LH arises after; subdues 3 kings; blasphemes, persecutes, changes laws; 3½ times (1260 days, or years)
	UNTIL	BUT	UNTIL	BUT
GOD WINS	Thrones set up; Ancient of Days takes seat; Court sits and books opened; Beast slain and burnt; Rest lose dominion; Lives extended for season; Jesus gets dominion + Dominion forever over all	Saints receive kingdom; Saints possess kingdom	Ancient of Days comes; Judgment in favor of saints; Time arrives when saints take kingdom	Court sits for judgment; LH dominion removed; Saints receive LH's dominion + God's kingdom ever over all
ANALYSIS	Notice tight chronological sequence: "I kept looking," denoting continuous sequence: 1st, 2d, another, 4th, LH, until. Judgment *after* reign of LH, yet *before* its punishment of destruction.	Nutshell interpretation: Beasts arise to steal God's dominion. When Jesus receives dominion, saints get kingdom. End result focuses on saints, not LH.	Judgment means of transferring kingdom from LH to saints. Again, end result is focused upon saints, not LH.	LH now explained in detail. Judgment follows *after* 1260 but *before* LH loses power. Result of judgment: Saints get dominion from LH. Ultimately, it is God's kingdom (1 Cor. 15:24-28). Saints are joint heirs with His Son (Rom. 8:17).

Nutshell interpretation:

peoples, nations, and men of every language might serve Him' " (verse 14). *Since a result of the judgment is that Christ receives rulership, it is evident that His right to govern was under question.* The open books have shown God to be fair. Calvary's love has indeed been consistently extended to everyone alike throughout history. The Shepherd has been good.

2. The establishment of Christ's rulership means *the defeat of Satan's challenge.* In Daniel 2:21 we read that God " 'changes the times and the epochs,' " but through the devil's agent the little horn, Satan has been attempting to "change times and laws" (chap. 7:25, K.J.V.). While correctly identifying the historic Antichrist, many of us have overlooked the principle underlying the government of this little horn. It is humbling to learn that we partake of its spirit if we refuse to live in faith and to trust that "my times are in Thy hand" (Ps. 31:15). When seeking to direct our own lives, we participate in the atrocities of Antichrist, who seeks to substitute himself and his works in the place of God and His work. We do this not only in pursuing sin but also by erecting a graven image of personal righteousness in competition with Calvary. In the endorsement of Christ's right to rule and save, we condemn all that is outside of faith in His righteousness (see John 3:18), including the devil and his legalistic little horn.

3. *The saints are vindicated* and receive a favorable verdict (Dan. 7:22). When God and His salvation activities are endorsed, the eternity of those who are hid with Christ in Him is automatically upheld. When it is shown that we indeed have chosen to believe in Jesus, we are officially included in His victory. We are delivered from the accusations and persecutions of the little horn and its originator. God had considered us righteous in Christ all along, but this is His official defense in court of our relationship with Him.

Definitely Biblical

In summary, the Bible is clear in evidence both abundant and indisputable that there would be an investigation to (1) vindicate God's rulership, (2) condemn unbelievers, and (3) endorse the innocent standing of the saints. Daniel 7 further proves that this judgment would take place after the reign of the little horn was interrupted in 1798, just before the glorious coming of the kingdom. What is more, the prophetic base for this doctrine was endorsed centuries before us by the Protestant Reformation.

Simply stated, the post-Ascension, pre-Advent judgment is definitely Biblical.

6 The Dilemma of Daniel 8

S even score and more years ago our forefathers brought forth upon this continent a new movement, conceived in prophecy and dedicated to the proposition that Christ is coming soon. Now we are engaged in a great civil war, testing whether this movement—the only one so conceived and so dedicated—can long endure. Our flag has hung at half-mast. Apostasy has hijacked our blessed hope. One hundred shepherds have forsaken the flock of truth. Thousands of loyal members now wonder what the church is coming to. The time has come for patriots of truth to stand up again and be counted once again as the people of the Book. Quickly we must arise and shine in such a time as this. Let freedom reign!

In the 1860s America was struggling for survival. Rebellion had challenged our existence as a free and united republic. Bloody battles were ravaging our resources and sapping our spirit. Under the cloudy skies of Gettysburg, President Abraham Lincoln addressed the national crisis in a stark and simple speech we will never forget. If Lincoln were alive today as a Seventh-day Adventist, he might describe our situation in similar terms with a "Glacier View Address."

Glacier View, you may recall, is an Adventist campground nestled more than nine thousand feet high in the Colorado Rockies. Its peaceful, pastoral setting belied the turbulence of August, 1980, when a jury of 114 church administrators, scholars, and pastors convened there for an investigative judgment of the challenge raised by Desmond Ford. Ten months previously, Ford had undermined the prophetic platform of Adventism in a speech before a forum at Pacific Union College. Ford was quite thorough and persuasive. Verdict Publications, a dissident organization, duplicated tapes of the talk and whirled them around the world.

The effects were immediate and devastating. Thousands of solid members who had always stood straight in the Adventist message doubled over with doubt. Some of the church's finest young pastors quit. There were demands that Ford be recalled for structural defects in his doctrine. Ford thought he had a better idea about how to interpret Adventist pillars, but church leaders disagreed. He was suspended from responsibilities at Pacific Union College and given six months to prepare for a thorough evaluation of his theology at Glacier View.

Although some points were conceded to Dr. Ford at the conference, his basic premises were rejected. Shortly thereafter Ford was fired, and his ordination has since been canceled. Although Ford no longer speaks with church authority, his penetrating questions still confront the consciences of many thoughtful Adventists.

In the center of the storm at Glacier View was the dilemma posed by Daniel 8:14: " 'For 2,300 evenings and mornings; then the holy place will be properly restored.' " Key questions the brethren wrestled with in this text were: What are these 2,300 evenings and mornings? Which sanctuary is indicated here? What is involved in its restoration, and when does this take place?

Even more basically, Who is the little horn that wreaks havoc in the sanctuary and necessitates its restoration?

Antiochus Again?

Ford contended that, first and primarily, this blasphemous culprit is Antiochus Epiphanes. Does the Greek ruler fit into Daniel 8 after he failed to fulfill in Daniel's previous prophecy? A number of facts expel Antiochus from extended consideration here:

1. Antiochus did not appear at " 'the latter period' " (verse 23) of the Greek dynasty, "but approximately in the middle of the line of Seleucid kings. (The Seleucid dynasty ran from 312/311 to 65 B.C., and Antiochus Epiphanes reigned from 175 to 164 B.C."[1]

2. It is not true that Antiochus "grew exceedingly great" (verse 9). His father had restored the original Seleucid dominions and thus was called "the Great." Antiochus Epiphanes, on the other hand, was referred to sarcastically by some of his contemporaries as "Epimanes"—the madman.[2] His advance into Egypt was reversed by a mere warning from a Roman officer, and his expeditions finally resulted in his death.[3]

3. Antiochus also fails the test of time. The Temple was to be desolate until 2300 days had passed. This did not happen. Nothing Antiochus did can be stretched to fit here. To compensate for the shortfall, attempts are made to cut the time period in half, to 1150 days, and then link it to the time the king did pollute the Temple.[4] But when it is shown that not even 1150 days fit the events,[5] it is sometimes suggested that the time periods are not intended to be accurate.

But prophecy is "a lamp shining in a dark place, until the day dawns" (2 Peter 1:19). What is the purpose of the time scales if they are inaccurate and unreliable? That these numbers are meant to be quite precise is evident by the way the angel makes careful distinction between the 1290- and 1335-day periods in Daniel 12.

4. Another element that eliminates Antiochus is the climax of the Daniel 8 prophecy. It culminates in " 'the time of the end' " (verse 17), when the little horn " 'will be broken without human agency' " (verse 25). Antiochus died of natural causes nearly two centuries before the days of Christ. No stretch of the most fertile imagination can extend the career of Antiochus into the cosmic events at the

close of time.

The Adventist rejection of Antiochus as the fulfillment of Daniel 8 is endorsed by the words of Jesus in Matthew 24:15. There He projects the desolation wrought by the little horn to some future fulfillment. This position was formerly held by Desmond Ford himself in his 1978 commentary on Daniel: "The blasphemies and aggression associated by many with the Syrian king are applied by Christ in this discourse to a power soon to attack Jerusalem and precipitate a time of tribulation not only for the Jews as a nation but for all Christians everywhere."[6]

Since the forecast of Daniel 8 extended far into the future from Daniel's time, it is apparent that its 2300 days, like the 1260 days of Daniel 7, must be symbolic of years. This should be expected, since the context of Daniel's prophecies is figurative—short-lived animals illustrate centuries of national existence. While a full discussion of the day-year principle is reserved for chapter ten of this book, it is interesting to note that "as far back as 1205, an anonymous Joachimite work interpreted the number 2300 as 23 centuries from Daniel's time."[7]

Who is this desolating power, if not Antiochus? The true fulfillment of the little horn of Daniel 8 can only be Rome.

Rome Repeats

1. Rome came to power "'in the latter period'" (verse 23) of the Greek Empire.

2. In becoming a world power, Rome certainly "grew exceedingly great toward the south, toward the east, and toward the Beautiful Land [Palestine]" (verse 9). "Coming from the west, small at first like a 'little' [K.J.V.] horn, Rome grew as it conquered Macedonia in 168 B.C., Syria in 64 B.C., Palestine in 63 B.C., and Egypt, too, after a long protectorate, in 30 B.C., making them all provinces of its own empire."[8]

3. When viewed in both its pagan and papal phases, Rome does indeed extend until "'the time of the end'" (verse 17). When imperial Rome crumbled in the late fifth century A.D., the Roman Church became successor to the Roman emperor. C. Mervyn Maxwell quotes a recent college textbook to explain this fusion of pagan and papal Rome:

"In the West, the Church took over the defense of Roman civilization. The emperor gave up the [pagan] title of Pontifex maximus (high priest) because the Roman gods were no longer worshipped. The bishop of Rome assumed these priestly functions, and this is why the Pope today is sometimes referred to as the Pontiff. When the Huns, a fierce and savage tribe led by brutal Attila, swept into Italy and threatened to take and destroy the city of Rome, it was the leader of the Christian Church, Pope Leo, not the emperor, who met the barbarian. Attila was so impressed with the Pope's spiritual power that he turned back. What Leo said to Attila remains unknown, but what is significant is the fact that it was the Pope and not the emperor who stood at the gates of Rome. The Roman Empire had become the Christian Church."[9]

Since the Roman Church was a continuation of the Roman Empire, a single prominent horn appropriately represents both of them, and through the church the little horn of Rome still exists in this end of time.

4. Both pagan and papal Rome destroyed " 'the holy people' " (verse 24). Ford in 1978 noted that "the 'fearful destruction' [R.S.V.] mentioned in verse 24 fits imperial and papal Rome better than it does Antiochus. The latter killed 40,000 Jews when he took Jerusalem, but Rome destroyed many times more in A.D. 70, and the toll of the Middle Ages resulting from religious intolerance was far greater still." [10]

5. Both pagan and papal Rome "removed the regular sacrifice" and caused "the place of His [Christ's] sanctuary" to be "thrown down" (verse 11). According to Maxwell: "Pagan Rome did this literally—but only in a limited sense, as we shall see later—in A.D. 70, when soldiers under the Roman general (later emperor) Titus set the temple (or Jerusalem sanctuary) on fire, causing its complete destruction and forever terminating its services. In the 130s the Roman emperor Hadrian constructed a pagan temple in Jerusalem, renamed the city Aelia Capitolina, and went so far as to forbid Jews ever to live in the city—a rule that was enforced for centuries." [11]

War Against the Sanctuary

How did papal Rome fight against the sanctuary? First we must ask, What sanctuary is "thrown down" here by the papacy? The Bible reveals two sanctuaries—the earthly, or Jewish, Temple, and the heavenly sanctuary. After Jesus pronounced the earthly Temple desolate (Matt. 23:38), the torn veil (chap. 27:51) published its abandoned and obsolete condition. Its subsequent destruction endorsed the bankruptcy of the Jewish religious system. The New Testament redirects our focus away from that Temple and its priests on earth to our "high priest, who has taken His seat at the right hand of the throne of the Majesty in the heavens, a minister in the sanctuary, and in the true tabernacle, which the Lord pitched, not man" (Heb. 8:1, 2). Anything happening to God's sanctuary reaching to " 'the time of the end' " would have to involve this heavenly temple.

How did papal Rome throw down this heavenly sanctuary? According to the passage, there is a cosmic controversy, for the little horn "grew up to the host of heaven" (Dan. 8:10). The core of the conflict would be a struggle over doctrine, since it was to "fling truth to the ground" (verse 12). Specifically, the truth of Christ's "regular sacrifice" in "His sanctuary" (verse 11) would be attacked, and a counterfeit religious system would be set up on earth, in place of heaven's sanctuary, that would "perform its will and prosper" (verse 12).

What is the "regular sacrifice" taken away from Christ by the Roman Church? Actually, the Hebrew word here is *tamid* and means a "continual" something— without expressing what the something is. Translators have sometimes added the term *sacrifice* or *burnt offering* in an attempt to make the passage fit Antiochus

Epiphanes. But such unauthorized additions to the text take attention away from the "continual"—that is, the all-of-the-time high-priestly ministry of Jesus Christ on our behalf in the heavenly sanctuary, who "always [continually] lives to make intercession" for us (Heb. 7:25).

How did the Roman Church throw down the "continual" ministry of Jesus in the heavenly sanctuary? In obscuring the gospel of free grace with such perversions of salvation as (1) penance for sin after confessing to a human priest, (2) purgatory, (3) the veneration of Mary as "Mother of God," and the mass, which is purported to be "the same sacrifice as the sacrifice of the cross." [12] All this has hindered reliance upon the finished work of Christ on Calvary, extended to us through His ministry in the heavenly sanctuary, where He now "intercedes for us" (Rom. 8:34).

Daniel 8:13 asks, " 'How long ["Until when," literally] will the vision about the regular sacrifice apply, while the transgression causes horror, so as to allow both the holy place and the host to be trampled?' " In other words, Until what time will this sacrilegious sanctuary system function before its corruption is interrupted? This question is answered in the following verse: " 'For 2,300 evenings and mornings; then the holy place will be properly restored.' " Although suffering setback by this restoration of the sanctuary, the little horn expands operation until the coming of Christ finally puts it out of business (see verse 25).

Restoration of the Sanctuary

Now we may inquire, What does it mean for the sanctuary to be " 'properly restored' "? It will benefit us to compare the parallel events of chapters 7 and 8 in Daniel:

DANIEL 7	INTERPRETATION	DANIEL 8
Lion	Babylon	(Omitted—Babylon about to fade from importance)
Bear	Medo-Persia	Ram
Leopard	Greece	Goat
Dragon (1st phase)	Rome (political)	Little horn (1st phase)
Dragon (2d phase: little horn)	Rome (religious)	Little horn (2d phase)
Persecution	Dark/Middle Ages	Persecution
Judgment	Investigative judgment	Sanctuary restored
Little horn condemned/destroyed	End of time	Little horn condemned/destroyed

Notice that the judgment of Daniel 7 compares with the restoration of the sanctuary in the next chapter. There must be a connection between the two activities. Could they represent the same event?

To find out let us refer again to Daniel 8:14. According to Willaim Shea, "those translations which have translated this verb [the Hebrew *nisdaq*] as 'restored' have come closest to the original basic meaning of the verbal root involved." [13] Then Shea answers the question as to how well this translation fits the context:

"Since something bad clearly did happen to the sanctuary in the verses preceding this reference, this basic root meaning can be used with perfectly good sense here, as reversing or setting right whatever bad had happened to the sanctuary. There is no need to go beyond this into less frequently attested extended meanings to bring good sense to this passage, and indeed they do not bring as good sense to it as this basic meaning does." [14]

Historically, Adventists have thought it necessary to ignore the question of Daniel 8:13 and go instead to Leviticus 16 in order to understand Daniel 8:14. This is because in Leviticus the cleansing of the sanctuary on the Day of Atonement is detailed. There is a legitimate link between the restoration of the sanctuary in Daniel 8 and the Day of Atonement in Leviticus 16 (chapter eleven of this manuscript will review this connection), but it is unnecessary to go outside of Daniel 8 to establish this pillar of Adventism. In the restoration of the damage done by the little horn we see every principle of the Daniel 7 judgment.

Let us review those three elements from Daniel 7:

1. Christ's right to rule is vindicated as He receives the kingdom.

2. The little horn has its challenge defeated. Its dominion is taken away when the kingdom is restored to Christ and given to the saints.

3. The saints receive a favorable verdict and officially become part of His kingdom.

Each of these points is repeated in Daniel 8. "In the cleansing, restoring, righting, and emerging victorious of the heavenly sanctuary, there is a strong element of vindication of both God and His people." [15] Since the sanctuary is the headquarters of salvation activity, it involves both the forgiven and the condemned, as well as the fairness of the One who decides what occurs. Furthermore, the little horn has challenged the whole process of salvation by faith with a system of works mediated by a human priesthood. This is rejection of Christ's intercession in heaven's sanctuary. The restoration of the sanctuary, therefore, must bring the following results:

1. God's government of grace in the sanctuary is vindicated as the challenge against Christ's right to be the only mediator is defeated.

2. The establishment of God's system of salvation displaces the little horn's rival counterfeit. Salvation by works is condemned, along with its adherents.

3. The saints, who were condemned and persecuted by the little horn, are vindicated with their Mediator when their accuser loses his case in court.

The restoration of the sanctuary would also include a recovery of the truths that were "'trampled'" (Dan. 8:13) for so long. This would enable the saints, in the freedom of forgiveness without penance, to "keep the commandments of God and their faith in Jesus" (Rev. 14:12). Then the church will possess both the knowledge and the stimulus to enlighten the world with the true gospel. All these blessings were foretold in the assurance that the sanctuary would be "'restored.'"

For long ages Rome obscured the meaning of Christ's heavenly ministry. The dawning of the Reformation broke this spell of darkness, but not for several centuries more did God make provision for full brightness to be restored. The shining glory of the gospel in its full sanctuary setting will bring the final cosmic test. After every soul chooses between the darkness of Rome's counterfeit and the light of Christ's truth, the little horn "'will be broken'" (verse 25) by Christ Himself at His coming.

An Interrupted Visit

One final question remains: Precisely when can the 2,300-year period end and the sanctuary be restored? Daniel 8 states only that the time span stretches "'to the time of the end'"—it provides no starting point for this prophecy. The chapter ends abruptly as the aged prophet succumbs to emotional exhaustion (verse 27). Evidently he could not bear the bad news about the little horn. The angel Gabriel had to leave before his mandate to "'give this man an understanding of the vision'" was carried out. So Daniel did not yet comprehend the meaning of the vision concerning the 2300 days (verse 27).

In 1978 Desmond Ford suggested that Daniel 9 completes the unfinished business of this chapter: "Did Gabriel ever fulfill his commission? Did he complete his explanation of the vision? Where should we look, if not in the next chapter? In chapter 9 we find the prophet praying about the very matter left unexplained—the restoration of the sanctuary." [16]

To Daniel 9 we shall now go.

7 Worth Its Wait in Gold

One of the brightest minds of human history belonged to Sir Isaac Newton, an Englishman who three centuries ago revolutionized the study of science. Most famous for explaining the operation of gravity, Newton is also appreciated (except, of course, by some high school students) for the invention of calculus. Many acclaim his *Mathematical Principles of Natural Philosophy* to be one of the most important books ever written. Its composition in the short space of eighteen months is a scientific feat perhaps unsurpassed.

Newton's genius extended into other fields as well. A devout believer in the existence of God and His sovereign plan for this planet, Newton was an earnest student of Bible prophecy. In fact, he was a forerunner of the Adventist position on prophecy. His scholarship in the book of Daniel is especially impressive.

Daniel 9, according to Newton, contains "the foundation stone of the Christian religion."[1] Its precise predictions of the Messiah's appearance and accomplishments have fascinated and affirmed believers since the early centuries of Christianity. Furthermore, the connection linking Daniel 9 with the prophecy of the previous chapter is the cornerstone of a unique doctrine of Seventh-day Adventists. The next three chapters of this book will explore the evidence for the Adventist position on Daniel 9 and will address various challenges against this delightful and crucial Christ-centered jewel of the Old Testament.

Unfinished Business

At the close of Daniel 8 we left the prophet in deep distress, unable to understand the revelation. Evidently he feared the worst. Chapter 9 finds him near the end of his hope, engaging in earnest prayer. He is pouring out his heart to God in concern for the " 'desolate sanctuary' " (verse 17), which had been ravaged by Babylon some sixty-eight years before[2] and now lay in ruins. He begs God, " 'Do not delay, because Thy city and Thy people are called by Thy name' " (verse 19). What " 'delay' " is the prophet concerned about?

Daniel had discovered in the prophecies of Jeremiah that the desolation of Jerusalem was to last for seventy years (verse 2), after which the captive nation would be restored to Jerusalem (Jer. 25:11, 12; 29:10). But now with his people on the verge of freedom, a delay appears imminent.

Jeremiah had warned that God's promises were conditional upon the spiritual attitude of His people (chap. 18:7-10). The Jewish nation was in trouble because they had rebelled and refused to trust Him (Dan. 9:11, 12). Now, as Daniel observes the continued wickedness and " 'open shame' " (verse 7) of his people, he fears that God would have to delay their deliverance to the Promised Land. This happened in the days of Moses and Joshua. Daniel's apprehension increases as he remembers his vision received some ten years' previously, when the angel Gabriel informed him of a long time of trouble ahead for the saints and their sanctuary. It had been predicted that " 'both the holy place and the host [were] to be trampled' " until 2,300 days had expired; " 'then the holy place will be properly restored' " (chap. 8:13, 14).

Horrified at the atrocities that God's people and His truth would suffer, the elderly prophet had temporarily succumbed. By the time he recovered, the angel had gone, leaving Daniel "astounded at the vision, and there was none to explain it" (verse 27).

All these years Daniel had wondered when this tribulation would occur. Now, because of the Jews' abiding wickedness, the dreaded events appear imminent. Instead of return and restoration, a deeper crisis seems to threaten. Heartbroken, Daniel seeks God "with fasting, sackcloth, and ashes" (chap. 9:3).

" 'O Lord, in accordance with all Thy righteous acts, let now Thine anger and Thy wrath turn away from Thy city Jerusalem, Thy holy mountain; for because of our sins and the iniquities of our fathers, Jerusalem and Thy people have become a reproach to all those around us. So now, our God, listen to the prayer of Thy servant and to his supplications, and for Thy sake, O Lord, let Thy face shine on Thy desolate sanctuary. O my God, incline Thine ear and hear! Open Thine eyes and see our desolations and the city which is called by Thy name; for we are not presenting our supplications before Thee on account of any merits of our own, but on account of Thy great compassion. O Lord, hear! O Lord, forgive! O Lord, listen and take action! For Thine own sake, O my God, do not delay, because Thy city and Thy people are called by Thy name' " (verses 16-19).

Despite the desperate situation, Daniel's supplications are mingled with hope and even confidence. He knows that God loves His people and is eager to forgive. Furthermore, God had commanded Gabriel to " 'give this man an understanding of the vision' " (chap. 8:16). This mandate to Gabriel was a promise to Daniel that had not yet been fulfilled. That part of the vision that concerned the 2300 days and the desolate sanctuary was yet a mystery. Now the answer comes:

"Now while I was speaking and praying, and confessing my sin and the sin of my people Israel, and presenting my supplication before the Lord my God in behalf of the holy mountain of my God, while I was still speaking in prayer, then the man Gabriel, whom I had seen in the vision previously, came to me in my extreme weariness about the time of the evening offering. And he gave me instruction and talked with me, and said, 'O Daniel, I have now come forth to give you insight with understanding' " (chap. 9:20-22).

Although Daniel's prayer is comprised of confession and faith, we must keep in mind the reason he gave his attention to seek the Lord—the timing of the restoration of the Jews and their sanctuary.[4] Daniel prays, " 'Do not delay' " (verse 19). He is concerned about the calculation of time, and as Gabriel comes to give him " 'understanding of the vision' " (verse 23), he begins with an explanation of time: " 'Seventy weeks have been decreed for your people and your holy city, to finish the transgression, to make an end of sin, to make atonement for iniquity, to bring in everlasting righteousness, to seal up vision and prophecy, and to anoint the most holy place" (verse 24).

Six Goals for the Gospel

Here was good news. God in His grace would decree an extra span of probationary time for the Jews and their capital city, in order to accomplish six special goals:

1. " 'To finish the transgression.' " *Finish* in the Hebrew text comes from a root word meaning "to restrain."[5] *Transgression* here implies high-handed sin, willful transgression of known law. God gave the Jews this time as a final opportunity to reform their rebellious national attitude in answer to Daniel's prayer.

2. " 'To make an end of sin.' " "It is used in the plural and without the article, which means that it refers to sins and not sin offerings."[6] *Make an end* means "be complete, finished."[7] The same Hebrew term is translated "completed" in Lamentations 4:22: "The punishment of your iniquity has been completed, O daughter of Zion; He will exile you no longer." (See also Deut. 34:8 and Dan. 8:23.) Just as a completion was promised for the seventy years of exile, so an end would be made to the nation's guilt in missing the mark of God's glorious holiness. The basis of this provision is explained next.

3. " 'To make atonement for iniquity.' " Now we have come to the basic goal of the seventy weeks—atonement. "The verb used is the technical word, 'the offering of an atoning sacrifice.' In this sense it occurs some fifty times in Leviticus."[8] "A once-for-all element is implied for the particular atonement referred to here in this prophetic context."[9] "It is announcing that God has found a way of forgiving sin without being untrue to His own righteousness. This assurance was what the prayer had been feeling after; it was the great longing expressed in the Old Testament as a whole."[10]

4. " 'To bring in everlasting righteousness.' " Translated literally, this means "to bring in righteousness of ages."[11] The removal of a condemned building is not enough to meet the needs of its occupants—a new dwelling must be built in its place. Not only would God bulldoze away the wretched ruins of sin with the making of atonement; He would also provide an eternal monument of righteousness within which His saints can live and move and have their being.

5. " 'To seal up vision and prophet.' "[12] Two possible interpretations vie for endorsement here: first, that the seventy weeks in some way would seal, or confirm, the whole vision of Daniel 8 and its ongoing significance. "In a special

sense the events of the seventy weeks guarantee the fulfillment of the particular promise of the previous vision—'then the sanctuary shall be restored' (chap. 8:14 [R.S.V.]). The accomplishment in history of the events of the 490 years ratify, or make certain, the accomplishment of what has been promised for the period following the 2300 years.' "[13]

A second possible interpretation is that the ministry of prophetic vision to the Jewish nation would end with the conclusion of the seventy weeks. Shea endorses this latter interpretation. He sees "the meaning of sealing or shutting up in the sense of bringing to an end. . . . This would mean that for that city and people prophet and vision were to cease by the end of the time period prophesied. This could have been either for their weal or woe. If they developed the righteous society which Daniel and the other prophets called for and envisioned, then the restoration of the kingdom with all the peace, prosperity, and righteousness seen flowing from it could have been brought about. Vision and prophet would no longer have been necessary then because all that the classical prophets had talked about would have been fulfilled. If they did not comply with the desired conditions, however, then the prophetic voice and vision among them would cease since God would no longer speak to them in this way."[14]

Although both interpretations appear to be permitted by the context, the latter seems to harmonize better with the parallel phrases in Daniel 12:4, 9. Additionally, the stoning of Stephen at the close of this period of probation lends support to this second interpretation:

"The reference to 'prophet' here seems strange since one would have expected the word 'prophecy' to appear here instead. Looking back at this phrase from Stephen's experience, however, it can be viewed in a new light. Stephen was the last true prophet whom God called to that office to speak particularly to the people of His election. When their leaders stoned him they silenced the voice of the last in a long line of their prophets. His death brought an end to the function of the prophetic office on their behalf as a people. The vision that he saw just before he died was the last vision that a prophet who ministered especially to them was to see. As far as Daniel's own particular people were concerned, vision and prophet had been sealed up. From this time forward the prophetic gift was to be manifested in the arena of Christ's Church instead.' "[15]

6. " 'To anoint the most holy place.' " [16] Which temple is involved here? "It could not have been the second temple built in Jerusalem since it was dedicated for use when its construction was completed in 515 B.C. (Ezra 6:15-18). The destruction of that temple was predicted two verses later in this passage [Dan. 9:26] and it contains no further reference to any subsequent reconstruction of it after its destruction. Thus the temple to be anointed according to this prophecy was not the second temple and no third temple in Jerusalem was envisioned. By a process of elimination, therefore, the holy place or temple referred to here must be in heaven and its anointing must have taken place when Christ ascended to heaven."[17]

So the sanctuary in heaven would be anointed. What could this mean? "The word *anoint* can signify a material anointing with sacred oil; or better, a spiritual anointing with the idea of consecration or dedication of the sanctuary." [18]

In Exodus 40:1-15 we see that to begin the yearly cycle of events in the Old Testament sanctuary, the building and its furnishings were anointed, dedicated for service. Following this, the high priest and his sons were themselves anointed, in order to "'qualify them for a perpetual priesthood throughout their generations'" (verse 15). Therefore "the anointing of the earthly sanctuary was a ritual that took place with a view to beginning the priestly ministration in the sanctuary." [19] Evidently the anointing of the heavenly sanctuary foretold here by Daniel would begin a new priestly ministry before God's throne.

In these six items of promise we have God's remedy for the sin problem Daniel was praying about. In Heaven's eternal mercy a specified span of further probation was given to the nation, during which sin would be atoned for and replaced with eternal righteousness. The initiation of a new priesthood in heaven's temple would follow these accomplishments.

Job Description for Jesus

It should be quickly obvious to every Christian that we have in the six points of the Daniel 9 prophecy a thrilling forecast of the work of Christ:

1. Jesus pleaded with His rebellious people to "'repent and believe in the gospel'" (Mark 1:15). In spite of His attempts to restrain their transgression, "those who were His own did not receive Him" (John 1:11).

2. Jesus proclaimed in triumph as He died, "'It is finished!'" (chap. 11:30). His atoning sacrifice was completed and accomplished. We are all sinful and incomplete in our character development, but on the cross Christ conquered "'to make an end'" to our guilt in missing the mark.

3. By the death of Jesus "we have redemption through His blood, the forgiveness of our trespasses" (Eph. 1:7). Full sacrificial atonement was provided "to reconcile all things to Himself, having made peace through the blood of His cross" (Col. 1:20).

4. Through Jesus' atoning death for our sin God "has qualified us to share in the inheritance of the saints in light. For He delivered us from the domain of darkness, and transferred us to the kingdom of His beloved Son, in whom we have redemption, the forgiveness of sins" (verses 12-14). In legal terms God "raised us up with Him, and seated us with Him in the heavenly places, in Christ Jesus" (Eph. 2:6). Since He became "the source of eternal salvation" (Heb. 5:9), Christ fulfilled the promise of Daniel 9:24 "'to bring in everlasting righteousness.'"

5. Christ also sealed up both vision and prophet in His closing days of ministry. He cried, "'O Jerusalem, Jerusalem, who kills the prophets and stones those who are sent to her! How often I wanted to gather your children together, the way a hen gathers her chicks under her wings, and you were unwilling'" (Matt. 23:37). He promised them even more prophets, "'some of them you will

kill and crucify, and some of them you will scourge in your synagogues, and persecute from city to city, that upon you may fall the guilt of all the righteous blood shed on earth'" (verses 34, 35). For rejecting these final messengers, their nation would be forsaken and "'desolate'" (verse 38). No more prophets and their visions would minister to them.

6. After Jesus "obtained eternal redemption" "He entered the holy place" (Heb. 9:12) in heaven, where "He always lives to make intercession" for us (chap. 7:25). He is our "great high priest" at "the throne of grace," where "we may receive mercy and may find grace to help in time of need" (chap. 4:14, 16). The emergence of Christ's new priesthood in the heavenly sanctuary proves the fulfillment of the promise that the Most Holy Place would be anointed.

Worth Waiting For

We have examined a remarkable prediction of the work of Christ. How strange that some should look to Antiochus Epiphanes rather than to Jesus as the focus of this forecast of atonement. With the definite evidence that Daniel 9 centers around the Saviour, we need not exhume the corpse of Antiochus for yet another wasted autopsy.[20]

The dramatic visit of the angel reported in this chapter brought great relief to the prophet. For a decade after the vision of the 2300 days, Daniel had feared the worst for his people. Finally he received peace of mind—and more. Not only would the captive nation be restored to their homeland but they would be crowned with their Messiah!

This wonderful news was a long time in coming. But it was *worth its wait in gold.*

8 Farewell, Adventism?

C hristmas Eve, 1981, a bomb was dropped on the Anaheim Adventist church. It came in the form of a letter from Steve, one of the deacons. There was no longer room in his heart for the Adventist faith. He had seen some star that was leading him out of the church. In his public epistle entitled "Farewell, Adventism," Steve went right to the point: "I have switched my faith from Seventh-day Adventism to the New Testament faith."

Frequently in years past I had heard it said that nobody seemed to leave the Adventist Church over doctrine (except, of course, for some heretics around the turn of the century). Often, when someone did leave, the problem was diagnosed as an unwillingness to walk the straight and narrow. Or, more perceptively, our autopsy blames spiritual suicide on the lack of a relationship with Christ.

Things have changed since recent doctrinal tornadoes have swept through the church. Many thoughtful Adventists are deeply troubled about their church's teachings. Some, like Steve, have left. But most stay on, perhaps lacking the courage or direction to go elsewhere.

What is wrong? Each case is different, naturally, but often the troubled waters swirl around the year 1844. Steve, for example, could not accept that 2,300 years before the great Disappointment something happened to begin the fulfilling of the prophecy of Daniel 9. In his goodbye letter he insisted that "the Adventist must again and again use unprovable presuppositions and leap across big chasms of nonexistent evidence. . . . Adventists cannot prove that the 2300 . . . days must begin in 457 B.C. The common person cannot follow the flow of argument without great difficulty, and no reputable Bible scholar has ever given it a second thought."

If Steve is correct, one has no reason to be a Seventh-day Adventist. Actually, back in 1979 I shared the same doubts. These next two chapters will explain how my fragmented confidence in the Adventist interpretation of Daniel 9 has been welded into firm conviction that the position regarding 1844 is Biblically legitimate. The goal of this chapter is to recognize the foundation of 1844 in the prophecy of the seventy weeks in Daniel 9. Several things we must learn are (1) who ordered the decree to restore Jerusalem, (2) when this decree was carried out, and (3) how the baptism and death of Jesus certified later events foretold by Daniel 8 and 9. This leaves opportunity for our next chapter to bring us up to the nineteenth century and 1844.

We have already seen that the angel Gabriel assured Daniel that his people would rebuild and restore Jerusalem, finally witnessing the saving sacrifice of their Messiah. In that same visit Gabriel also disclosed the prophetic time frame for these promised blessings. As impressive as this Daniel 9 passage is in predicting the accomplishments of Christ, it is even more striking for its accuracy in forecasting the time of His appearing.

A total term of seventy weeks (units of seven) is involved here, counting "'from the issuing of a decree to restore and rebuild Jerusalem'" (verse 25). First we must know who ordered this decree.

Royal Friends of God's People

Three decrees must be considered. All are recorded in the book of Ezra.

"1. The first of these three decrees, issued in 538 (or possibly 537) by Cyrus the Great, permitted a resettlement of the Jewish exiles in their homeland and empowered them to build for God 'a house at Jerusalem.' Ezra 1:2-4 [R.S.V.]. In connection with this decree Cyrus released the sacred utensils that Nebuchadnezzar had carried to Babylon—and which Belshazzar had blasphemously drunk from on the night when Cyrus defeated him, only a year or two prior to this decree. There were 5,469 of them. Ezra 1:7-11.

"Some fifty thousand Jews returned to Palestine within a year. They ran into stiff opposition from the non-Jewish inhabitants of the area. The record in the books of Ezra and Nehemiah sounds almost like a modern newscast from the Middle East!

"In the face of this opposition, work on the temple dragged (see Ezra, chapters 2 to 5).

"2. The second of the three decrees was issued around 519 by Darius I Hystaspes (not to be confused with Darius the Mede). Shortly after Darius began to reign, he received a letter asking him to confirm the original decree made by Cyrus. Darius ordered a thorough search of the Persian archives in Babylonia and Ecbatana, and when an official memo of the decree was at last recovered (Ezra 6:1-5), he cheerfully issued the requested confirmation (Ezra 6:6-12).

"3. The third decree was issued by Artaxerxes I Longimanus."[1]

Under Cyrus the rebuilding began, and was finished under Darius (verse 15). But Artaxerxes restored, or adorned (chap. 7:27), the completed Temple.

"Qualitatively, this third decree (Ezra 7:11-26) was superior to the first two, for it commissioned Ezra to appoint magistrates and judges with full political and religious authority to try cases under both Jewish and Persian law and to impose capital punishment."[2]

Not until this final order was Jerusalem restored as the national capital. This explains why the three decrees are listed as a single unit in Scripture: "They finished building according to the command of the God of Israel and the decree of Cyrus, Darius, and Artaxerxes king of Persia" (chap. 6:14).

To illustrate this point, let us imagine that Cyrus began building a house and Darius finished its construction. But not until Artaxerxes issued the occupation permit could the building be used. Therefore, we must date the rebuilding and restoration from the order of the third king.

Some protest consideration of the command of Artaxerxes as fulfillment of the prophecy "'to restore and rebuild Jerusalem.'" Robert Brinsmead, for example, quotes the following in his book *Judged by the Gospel*: "But there is *not one word* in the letter [of Artaxerxes] or the context about building anything. . . . Artaxerxes had authorized Ezra to start a religious reform, not build a city."[3]

Such critics err in limiting Daniel 9 to involve merely building construction. They overlook that the promise included restoration, as well as rebuilding. The desolation of Jerusalem that distressed Daniel included much more than the destruction of buildings. The privilege of Jerusalem to function in administrating God's laws had been removed, so the restoration of the city would require the reestablishment of civil and religious government. This was accomplished by the decree of Artaxerxes as the fulfillment of Daniel 9. Through the past centuries many scholars from divergent backgrounds have understood this.[4] A recent book that has been widely advertised and acclaimed among evangelicals, *Encyclopedia of Bible Difficulties*, likewise links Artaxerxes' decree in Ezra 7 with Daniel 9.[5]

Beginning the Rebuilding

Now we must find out the date of this decree so we can know from what point to count the seventy weeks. We learn from Ezra 7 that this happened in the seventh year of Artaxerxes. Ezra arrived in Jerusalem to carry out the king's order in the fifth month of that year (verses 7, 8). "The seventh year of Artaxerxes I is now firmly established as 458/457 B.C., with the return of Ezra in 457, and not 458 B.C.,"[6] as some had suggested. "The fifth month of the seventh year of Artaxerxes fell in the late summer or early autumn of 457 B.C., and the decree was implemented soon afterward."[7] This date has been proven beyond reasonable doubt by archeological discoveries in 1947[8] and is being acknowledged by scholars today.[9]

So the seventy weeks that would bring in the Messiah began in the autumn of 457 B.C. It is quickly obvious that "a week of days could not have been meant inasmuch as the events foretold could never have been fulfilled within 490 days, particularly the rebuilding of the city that was allotted seven weeks only."[10] The Hebrew word here in Daniel 9 translated "weeks" "simply denotes a unit of seven, and may designate a period of either seven days or seven years."[11] "There is virtually unanimous agreement among interpreters of all schools of thought that the phrase 'seventy weeks' or literally 'sevens seventy' . . . means 490 years."[12]

Of these seventy weeks of years, the first sixty-nine heptads ("series of seven")[13] are supposed to bring us to the time of "'Messiah the Prince'" (verse 25). Did this indeed happen? According to the *Encyclopedia of Bible Difficulties*, "if, then, the decree of 457 granted to Ezra himself is taken as the terminus a quo for the commencement of the 69 heptads, or 483 years, we come out to the precise year of the appearance of Jesus of Nazareth as Messiah (or Christ): 483 minus 457 comes out to A.D. 26. But since a year is gained in passing from 1 B.C. to A.D. 1 (there being no such year as *zero*), it actually comes out to A.D. 27." [14]

We ought to note here that, up to this point of the prophecy, this evangelical work of scholarship endorses the Adventist position.

Anointing the Messiah

Messiah means "anointed one." [15] Christ was anointed with the Holy Spirit at His baptism by John the Baptist "in the fifteenth year of the reign of Tiberius Caesar" (Luke 3:1, 22; cf. Acts 10:38). When reckoned inclusively, "Tiberius's fifteenth year began in September or October A.D. 27." [16]

Immediately after becoming anointed as Messiah, Christ announced that " 'the time is fulfilled, and the kingdom of God is at hand; repent and believe in the gospel' " (Mark 1:15). To what time was He referring? It could only have been the prophetic time of which Daniel wrote—the sixty-nine prophetic weeks, or 483 years, that were to reach to " 'Messiah the Prince.' " Certainly a prophetic fulfillment of amazing precision!

Countdown to Calvary

One more week of years remained for the people of the covenant after A.D. 27. What would happen next? " 'In the middle of the week he will put a stop to sacrifice' " (Dan. 9:27). After a ministry of three and a half years, Jesus died on the cross as the Lamb of God. At the moment of death "the veil of the temple was torn in two from top to bottom" (Matt. 27:51). This signified the end of the Jewish sacrificial system.

Daniel's prophecy was further fulfilled in the manner of Christ's death: " 'Messiah will be cut off and have nothing ["no one," margin]' " (Dan. 9:26). Stripped bare by man and forsaken as cursed by His Father, Jesus had nothing and no one as He paid our ransom. Now we who were cursed and lost in our sins may have everything in Him. On our own account we are wretched, miserable, poor, blind, and naked. But in Christ we are rich, increased with goods, and in need of nothing. Praise be to God for His gospel of grace! And Daniel foretold it all five centuries in advance.

The date of the crucifixion has presented a question in interpreting this prophecy. Three and one-half years from the end of the sixty-nine heptads in the autumn of A.D. 27 is the spring of A.D. 31, the time required by Daniel 9. However, the majority of scholars see A.D. 30 as the more likely date. Is an A.D. 31 crucifixion possible according to evidence available?

Maxwell observes that "all commentators take into account that the crucifixion occurred, in general, while Pontius Pilate was procurator (A.D. 26-36) and, in particular, at a Passover that fell no more than three or four years later than His baptism. . . .

Those scholars who settle on the year 31 do so partly by appealing to astronomy. . . . But astronomers themselves insist that they cannot provide the information needed to settle the question of the calendar year of the cross! Either 30 or 31 is possible, they say, depending on a variety of factors."[17]

After presenting quite a thorough and persuasive argument, Maxwell points out that "a Friday crucifixion in A.D. 31 is entirely 'possible' according to astronomical calculations (for whatever they may be worth), granted a few unprovable yet reasonable assumptions."[18]

Maxwell concludes: "We are thus very certainly close to A.D. 31. A margin of error—if one should even think to call it an error—of only a single year in a prophecy spanning half a millennium would still be deeply impressive. It would represent less than one quarter of one percent! . . . But it isn't necessary to accept even this slight possible discrepancy."[19]

Given the remarkable precision of the 483-year time span, from 457 B.C. to A.D. 27, we find it only reasonable to accept the middle of Daniel's last week of years, the springtime of A.D. 31, as the date of our Lord's death for us.

In this chapter we have traced our prophetic roots back to 457 B.C. That year the clock of Daniel 9 began ticking toward the establishment of both Christianity and Adventism. Christ's timely baptism and sacrifice certified the chronological cornerstone that brought our church to birth in 1844. Our next section will focus on that long span of time between the crucifixion and the nineteenth century.

Fare Well!

Remember Steve? He dismembered himself from his church with the benediction "Farewell, Adventism." He was correct in a way he did not surmise. Adventism will indeed "fare well" as the mighty Spirit of truth sweeps through the earth to call out of Babylon those who will "keep the commandments of God and their faith in Jesus" (Rev. 14:12).

The remnant—those who remain after God purges this denomination and gathers His faithful into truth—may bear little resemblance to the church today. The promised revival of primitive godliness will bring many changes that will surprise us all.

But of one thing we may now be certain—the mighty pillars of truth will never be shaken. They are founded upon the solid Rock, Jesus Christ.

Are you?

9 Roots of the Holocaust

A uschwitz, Dachau, Ravensbrook—Hitler's death camps. Without question the atrocity of the century, perhaps of the millennium, is the Holocaust.

The systematic torture to death of innocent millions will haunt our hearts forever. The stench of corpses in cremation will always sting our memory. Like a pall of lingering smoke over a furnace, these many years later there are yet more questions around than answers. Questions about man and his gluttony for brutality. And questions about God and His love. More disturbing than the stark ruins of the death camps is the anguished cry—the angry demand—"*Why, God?* If this is how You treat Your friends, no wonder You have so many enemies!"

Who Is to Blame?

The Old Testament is a flower garden of God's expressed love and promised watchcare for the seed of Abraham, His children of choice. What happened? Did God forsake His family?

Or did they forsake Him? The Old Testament is also a thornbush, recording the constant rebellion, apostasy, and ingratitude of the Hebrew people. We have learned that in Daniel 9 God granted them 490 years of final opportunity to reform their wicked ways. But in A.D. 31, the middle of their last week of years, they murdered their own Messiah. Prophecy foretold this crime, and also those long centuries the gospel would be trampled upon by the little horn power. Finally, in 1844 God would provide final restoration of the truth that had been spurned by both the Jewish nation and the apostate Christian church. This chapter traces that long span of prophecy from the crucifixion to the mid-nineteenth century.

While pressing the reluctant Pilate to approve the killing of Christ, the Jews begged, "'His blood be on us and on our children!'" (Matt. 27:25). They requested full responsiblity for the consequences of their crime—not just for themselves, but for their posterity as well. This prayer was answered. The long history of Jewish surffering is rooted in their rejection of the Redeemer. Why, we wonder, should Jews today suffer for what their fathers did? But are we not all suffering for what Adam did?

When God created man and woman He decreed, "'Let them rule'" (Gen.

1:26). He knew that this power to influence the lives of those creatures under our care was quite a risk. Yet we would not represent His image, or could we be happy, without the gift of responsibility.

Certainly we are not liable for the sins of our ancestors (see Deut. 24:16). But we do reap the natural results of what they sowed. This may help us understand cancer, starvation, war, and the Holocaust.

After they "crucified the Lord of glory" (1 Cor. 2:8) the Jews still had the last half of the seventieth week of years in which to repent. (What a testimony to the mercy of God!) The 490 years of national probation, which began with the commandment to restore Jerusalem, would expire in the autumn of A.D. 34.

Murder of a Last Chance

What did God's covenant people do with their final opportunity? Christ gave them every chance, sending His apostles first to the city and nation that crucified Him. Although many responded (thousands on the day of Pentecost), the leaders spurned salvation. Messengers of warning were treated as traitors. Reading his fate in the frowns of the Jewish council, the martyr Stephen cried, " 'You men who are stiff-necked and uncircumcised in heart and ears are always resisting the Holy Spirit; you are doing just as your fathers did. Which one of the prophets did your fathers not persecute? And they killed those who had previously announced the coming of the Righteous One, whose betrayers and murderers you have now become' " (Acts 7:51, 52).

Stephen was stoned by the Sanhedrin, the highest governing body of the nation. In killing this first Christian martyr, they confirmed their rebellion against God. Finally they launched "a great persecution . . . against the church in Jerusalem" (chap. 8:1). Forced to flee, "those who had been scattered went about preaching the word" (verse 4).

During the three and a half years of probation remaining for God's chosen people after the cross, the gospel first had been preached especially to them. Now things changed. To the blaspheming Jews, Paul and Barnabas declared, " 'It was necessary that the word of God should be spoken to you first; since you repudiate it, and judge yourselves unworthy of eternal life, behold, we are turning to the Gentiles' " (chap. 13:46). The Jewish nation had rejected the probation promised in Daniel 9. After A.D. 34 the vineyard was given to new tenants (see Matt. 21:33-43).

If one event could symbolize the end of the Jews as God's chosen, it would probably be the execution of Stephen, which was followed shortly by the conversion of Paul, the apostle to the Gentiles. Shea contends that although we do not know for certain, A.D. 34 "remains a reasonable estimate for the date of the stoning of Stephen as derived from dates in the career of Paul." [1]

Actually it is not necessary to pinpoint any prescribed event to close the prophecy. Probation is conditional, so Gabriel did not say what particular fulfillment, if any, to expect in A.D. 34. By their response to the gospel the Jews would determine the finish of the 490 years. It is sufficient to note that the "six items [foretold in Daniel 9:24] were all legally accomplished by A.D. 34 at the end of the 490 years." [2]

The Price of Rebellion

Verse 26 of Daniel 9 warns of ultimate calamity that would befall the nation at a later date if Israel did not accept the probationary opportunity: " 'The people of the prince who is to come will destroy the city and the sanctuary. And its end will come with a flood; even to the end there will be war; desolations are determined.' " Just before the Jewish people climaxed their rejection of His ministry with murder, Jesus saw this desolation coming: " 'Behold, your house is being left to you desolate!' " (Matt. 23:38). He predicted that " 'all these things shall come upon this generation' " (verse 36).

Christ told the truth: "A few days before the A.D. 70 Passover, the Roman destroyers, under Titus, came to Jerusalem. They attacked the city and soon breached the wall. The city was overwhelmed. As the Temple precincts were entered, the daily sacrifices were stopped. The Temple was fired and destroyed, and the Jews ruthlessly slaughtered—their blood, according to Josephus, flowing in streams down the steps. The desolater had come. The city and Temple were in ruins; the desolation accomplished." [3]

After this, trouble for the Jews would continue " 'to the end' " (Dan. 9:26). Finally their persecutors would meet defeat, " 'even until a complete destruction, one that is decreed, is poured out on the one who makes desolate' " (verse 27). Ultimately only the kingdom of God will stand.

The "Gap Theory"

Besides the preterist theory of Antiochus that we discussed in a previous chapter, and the Messianic position that Adventists endorse, the futurists suggest a third interpretation of Daniel's seventy weeks—the "gap theory," with an antichrist to come. They separate the seventieth week from the rest of the prophecy by a gap of some two thousand years.

"Dispensationalists see this as the 'Church age,' which forms a 'parenthesis' between the first coming of Christ and the revived Roman empire whose prince will be the Antichrist. According to this view Daniel 9:24 is a programme for the future, not a summary of what took place in the work of Christ. Since the rebuilding of the Temple and the restoration of Jewish worship is envisaged according to this view, the official establishment of the state of Israel in 1948 has been greeted as heralding the events of the final week." [4]

Raymond Woolsey contests this gap theory:

"Some Bible students would take this seventieth week and separate it by more than two thousand years from the first sixty-nine. They say that it applies to a period yet future, after a supposed secret and invisible return of Christ, that it is a period when the Jews would again enjoy a special relationship with God.

However, the New Testament clearly states that the Christian church now stands before God as Israel. It is also absurd that in a time prophecy one should be so cavalier in dealing with time. Why specify 'seventy weeks,' or 490 years, when there would be that much plus more than two thousand years? Surely the seventieth week follows on the heels of the sixty-ninth week."[5]

More can be said: "The wording of the text in no way indicates a break or gap. . . . To insert into a 490-year period a 'gap' of two thousand years, four times longer than the entire 70 weeks itself, constitutes unwarranted manipulation. . . . This is a form of exegesis without a precedent in all prophetic exposition."[6]

A further problem for the futurists is their claim that the antichrist is to make the covenant (see Dan. 9:27) with the Jews. Mark Finley demonstrates that this is impossible: (1) the prophecy is Messianic, (2) there is no passage in the Bible where antichrist makes a covenant, and (3) the One who makes the covenant keeps it—not breaks it, as the futurists claim.[7]

In summary, "it seems abundantly clear to us that the specifications of the prophecy find exact and complete fulfillment in the life, ministry, and death of Christ, and in the subsequent desolation of the Jewish nation as a result of their rejection of the promised Messiah."[8]

A Clear Relationship

Now understanding the meaning of the 490 years in Daniel 9, let us consider once more its relationship with the 2300 years of Daniel 8. We have already seen the connection between the two prophecies—Daniel 9 is intended to explain the perplexities remaining in the prophet's mind when Gabriel departed before giving him "'an understanding of the vision'" (chap. 8:16). We noted that Daniel especially needed to understand the timing of the sanctuary's desolation. We must now learn when to begin counting the 2300 years.

No starting point for the 2300 years is given in Daniel 8. Could the two time periods, the 490 years and the 2300 years, run concurrently, one within the other?

According to *Ministry* magazine, "if the termination dates for these two time periods are not synchronous [that is, if they do not end at the same time], then the events described in the two prophecies cannot be identical or parallel in any sense of the word."[9]

Indeed, the events terminating these time periods are far separated. In Daniel 9 the anointing of the Most Holy Place is prior to Christ's service in the heavenly sanctuary. Daniel 9 was fulfilled at the time of the life and death of Jesus in the first century, while Daniel 8 focuses upon "'the time of the end'" (verses 17 and 19) of earth's history.

What, then, is the relationship between the 490 years and the 2300 years? The smaller is "cut off" from the larger. Regarding the word translated "'decreed'" (chap. 9:24), Desmond Ford in 1978 taught: "All Hebraists assert that its literal meaning is 'cut off.' The seventy weeks of years are 'cut off' from the longer period of 2300 years, and they commence with "'the going forth of the word to restore and build Jerusalem"' [R.S.V.]." [10] Ford quoted Phillip Newell's commentary: "The Hebrew word used here . . . has the literal connotation of 'cutting off' in the sense of severing from a larger portion." [11] *The Pulpit Commentary* agrees: "'Determined [K.J.V. for "'decreed'"],' as already indicated, means 'cut off.'" [12] The lexicon in *Strong's Concordance* concurs, along with *The New Brown, Driver, and Briggs Gesenius*. Ancient rabbinic literature employed a word that had "the sense of 'amputated.'" [13]

Doukhan perceives that "if the prophecy of Daniel 8 (*hāzōn*) points to a time of end, and if the prophecy of the 70 weeks indicates its starting point, then the period of the 70 weeks—which does not reach the end—must be understood as a smaller segment than the first one." [14]

Therefore, "the 490-year period would be cut off from the 2300-year period. The former would be for the Jews, the remainder would extend until the 'sanctuary be cleansed' [K.J.V.]. The baptism and crucifixion of Jesus and the gospel to the Gentiles occurred 'when the fulness of the time was come' (Gal. 4:4 [K.J.V.]), which assures us that we are on the right track in regard to the starting date and method of calculation. Hence we can with confidence calculate that the remainder of the 2300 years would extend to a.d. 1844. That was the time that the sanctuary was to be 'cleansed,' or 'vindicated'" [15]

Literal or Symbolic?

Some may question why the seventy weeks of years are taken literally, while the 2300 days are interpreted symbolically as a day for a year. *Questions on Doctrine* proposes an answer:

"A characteristic feature of symbolic prophecy is to give the component time periods, not literally, but in symbolic form. And it has been further demonstrated that Daniel 9:24-27 is a continuation of the literal explanation of the symbolic vision that was begun in Daniel 8:19-26. Now, inasmuch as Daniel 9:24-27 is a portion of the *literal explanation* of the symbolic vision, we would logically expect the time elements likewise to be given in literal terms." [16]

Adventism—the Logical Conclusion

In summary, a special work of restoring and vindicating the heavenly sanctuary was begun at the close of the 2300 years, in 1844.

Seventh-day Adventists, who stand alone among denominations in seeing prophetic significance in the year 1844, see their view as the "logical conclusion and climax of nearly a thousand years of progressive application of the year-day principle to the symbolic time periods of Bible prophecy. Its progenitors and champions have embraced literally hundreds of illustrious Jewish, Catholic, and Protestant scholars." [17]

Of the medieval Jews who interpreted the 2300 days as years, the ninth-century Nahawendi was first, joined by several more in the next century. No less than fifteen Jewish scholars before the sixteenth century supported this prophetic interpretation. [18]

Among Catholics, "About 1292 Arnold of Villanova said that *the 2300 days stand for 2300 years,* counting the period from the time of Daniel to the Second Advent. . . . Better known to most church historians is the illustrious Nicholas Krebs of Cusa, Roman Catholic cardinal, scholar, philosopher, and theologian, who in 1452 declared that the 2300 year-days began in the time of Persia." [19]

"In the century after the Protestant Reformation, many Protestant expounders, from English theologian George Downham (died 1634) to British barrister Edward King in 1798, declared the number 2300 involved the same number of years. John Tillinghast (died 1655) ended them at the second advent and the 1000-year reign of the saints. Tillinghast was *the first to assert the 70 weeks of years to be a lesser epoch within the larger period of the 2300 years.*" [20]

John Fletcher (Jean Guillaume de la Fléchère), an associate of John Wesley's, about 1755 interpreted the cleansing of the sanctuary as a restoration of truth from papal error at the end of a 2300-year period that began with Persia. [21]

And Johann Petri, a German Reformed pastor, "in 1768 introduced the final step . . . leading to the inevitable conclusion and climax—*that the 490 years (70 weeks of years) are the first part of the 2300 years.* He began them synchronously, 453 years before the birth of Christ—terminating the 49 years in a.d. 37, and the 2300 years in 1847. . . . Soon men on both sides of the Atlantic, in Africa, even in India and other countries, began to set forth their convictions in similar vein." [22]

Here is a fact the enemies of Adventism must note: Its prophetic structure existed long before the Millerite movement. Indeed, if the denomination is to be censured for its interpretations, so should the illustrious company of Biblical scholars who gave the church its prophetic heritage.

"They are our spiritual ancestors in this exposition, and we their logical successors and continuators. If we find ourselves differing with most fundamentalists and all modernists, that is because they have abandoned the historicist position—the one group for futurism, and the other for preterism. Our view represents the position once held by *their* spiritual ancestors." [23]

Conditional Confidence

The Seventh-day Adventist prophetic platform is not an innovation, but a restoration. Adventists simply honor the historic interpretations developed through the centuries by the Christian church, carrying them to their logical conclusions. Is it not reasonable to conclude that the church is God's worldwide movement of destiny?

But Adventists should not take carnal pride in their calling. There is no such thing as "once saved, always saved" for individuals or movements. Our only hope, personally and corporately, is in trusting the grace of God as we obey Him implicitly, and unreservedly follow the advancing light of truth.

The Jews regarded the promise of glorious triumph for their movement as proof that God's blessing would always be upon them. The fall of Jerusalem and the

Holocaust are tragic witness that they were fatally mistaken.

God's promises that involve human response are always conditional upon our obedient trust. With their rich prophetic heritage, it is easy for Adventists to become presumptuous, as did the first-century movement of destiny. A wealth of truth brings greater responsibility, not immunity.

God has waited a long time. Soon an overdue remnant (Rev. 12:17) will triumph over the cosmic forces of the little horn. Let us be faithful so we can be among them. We must trust and obey—there is no other way.

10 Mystery of the First Century

L ife-threatening adventure—such was Christianity in the century of its birth. As fatal fire storms of persecution swept through the church, thousands of brave martyrs were torched for the truth. Or slaughtered with the sword. Or torn by the teeth of lions—swiftly separated from brothers and sisters in Christ. As bereaved believers buried their beloved, no wonder their motto was "Maranatha!"—"The Lord is coming!"

Was this blessed hope a false alarm? The soon coming of Christ to their generation seems to be a dominant theme of New Testament authors. Was it an impossible dream?

Here is the problem: If the prophecies of Daniel project the Second Coming centuries after the cross, past 1844, what about "Maranatha"? How do we explain this expectancy of the early believers? How should we understand those New Testament passages that appear to assure the impending kingdom of Christ?

Much is at stake here for Adventists. How can the claim to be God's prophetic movement of destiny be sustained if Christ intended to end this world eighteen centuries before the Advent Movement began? This perplexity has forced many Adventists to falter in their remnant faith. It is absolutely crucial that we see this mystery solved. One of the following must be true:

Three Possibilities

(1) Daniel's prophecies were all designed to be fulfilled by the end of the first century, or (2) the New Testament does not permit the possibility of a first-century advent, or (3) if both of the above are false, then some harmony must be found for what seems to be a contradiction. In other words, if Daniel does extend until the end of time and the New Testament does permit a first-century return of Jesus, then we must reconcile a disagreement of nearly two thousand years in forecasting the end of the world.

Let us explore each of these possibilities in turn. First, was it possible for all of Daniel's prophecies to be fulfilled by the close of the first century?

This concept has already been crippled by ample evidence that these predictions stretch long past the first century unto " 'the time of the end' " (Dan. 8:17). The end of the world, according to Daniel 2, would not come until after the division of Rome, some four centuries following the days of the disciples. And Daniel 7, we have observed, weaves a tight chronological pattern predicting the breakup of a fourth world power, followed next by the reign of the little horn, then the judgment, and finally the coming of Christ's eternal kingdom. In Daniel 9 we marveled at the calendar countdown to the cross. Through the connection shared by that prophecy with Daniel 8 we have been brought to 1844 for the commencement of this preadvent judgment.

The Apotelesmatic Alternative

Certainly the historicist position of both Adventists and the Protestant pioneers accurately analyzes the prophecies of Daniel. However, it may be well at this point to address an alternative principle advanced by Desmond Ford, the "apotelesmatic" theory.

Throughout his Glacier View manuscript Ford teaches that all of Daniel's prophecies could have met fulfillment before the end of the first century.[1] With this apotelesmatic principle he attempts to refute evidence to the contrary. How? Ford explains: "By apotelesmatic we mean dual fulfillment or more."[2]

In other words, "simply stated, the apotelesmatic principle means that Biblical prophecies can have multiple fulfillments. To give an example, when the preterists interpret the 'little horn' [K.J.V.] as applying to Antiochus Epiphanes in second century B.C., when the historicists apply it to the papal rule of 1260 years, when the futurists apply it to an Antichrist that will enter Jerusalem sometime in the future, the apotelesmaticist will say that all three views are correct! 'All are right in what they affirm and wrong in what they deny,' states Ford (Glacier View manuscript, p. 505 [Daniel 8:14, the Day of Atonement, and the Investigative Judgment, p. 315])."[3]

Apparently, "the apotelesmatic principle is an umbrella that encompasses all the major schools of interpretation."[4] While it is certainly an imaginative theory, several major flaws stand against it:

"The apotelesmatic principle has no scriptural support. Dr. Ford does not offer any rationale as to how this 'principle' can be derived from Scripture; he just defines it, and then uses it."[5]

"The apotelesmatic principle does not give any clue as to when prophecy may have just one fulfillment . . . or multiple fulfillments. . . . If one scholar offers seven interpretations for a particular prophecy, and another seventy times seven, who is to say which one has gone too far and which one has stopped short of good exegesis?"[6]

"The apotelesmatic principle is unworkable with most Old Testament prophecies. If the principle is applied to one Messianic passage, namely Daniel 9:24-27, then for the sake of consistency it must be applied to all. How can one have a 'recurring fulfillment' of Micah 5:2? Is there going to be another incarnation, and is Bethlehem again to have significance? Are the events predicted in Psalm 22 and Isaiah 53 to be repeated? Is there going to be another Messianic figure who will vicariously suffer for the sins of his people?" [7]

Surely "it is clear that the apotelesmatic principle has no built-in control mechanism to prevent abundant speculation, making it impractical as an exegetical tool." [8]

When a Day Is a Year

Ford is much more convincing in his previous defense of the day-year principle in his 1978 commentary on Daniel:

"Inasmuch as short-lived beasts are employed as symbols of long-existent empires, it is most likely that the times mentioned are also presented to scale, with a small time unit representing a larger one." [9]

"The context of both Daniel 7 and 8 forbids the idea that the periods mentioned could be literal. In the first case the little horn emerges from the fourth world empire and endures till the time of the judgment and the advent, and 7:25 declares that the period of 'a time, two times, and half a time' [R.S.V.] extends over most of this time. How impossible this would be if three and a half years only were intended! Similarly, in 8:17 the prophet is told that the 2300 days would extend from the restoration of the sanctuary until 'the time of the end.' This means that a period of approximately 2300 years is involved. The treading down of the sanctuary brought to view in 8:11-13 could not begin before the restoration spoken of in 9:25, in the fifth century B.C. And besides this, its terminus is expressly stated as belonging to the latter days, just prior to the final proclamation of the gospel by the 'wise' (see 12:3, 4 [R.S.V.]). It has been largely overlooked by critics that 8:17, when linked with 12:3, 4, 9, 10, 13, makes it conclusive that the 2300-day period covers many centuries. Likewise in Revelation 12 the forty-two-month period covers the greater part of the time between the first and second advents, when the church would be in the wilderness of persecution during the Dark Ages. This is granted by almost all expositors. . . .

"Are there any indications in the rest of Scripture that God has ever chosen such [day for a year] symbolism? In Numbers 14:34 and Ezekiel 4:6 we find evidence that such is the case. God has chosen on other occasions to use precisely this symbolism; one of these occasions was during the time of Daniel's captivity, and its use was in connection with a contemporary prophet. . . .

"The pragmatic test should now be applied and the question asked: Have any of Daniel's prophecies already met with a precise fulfillment that accords with the principle we are studying? Daniel 9:24-27, the prophecy of the seventy weeks, seems to offer just such a fulfillment. . . . Inasmuch as other evidence shows that this period of 490 years is cut off from the longer period of the 2300, it is obvious that the latter must consist of years also. Thus here in Daniel 9 we have the pragmatic test met, and the year-day principle justified, despite the fact that the word *day* is nowhere used in this passage." [10]

Here we have quite a compelling defense by Ford of the day-year principle. One wonders how he could abandon such able scholarship to adopt the dubious and unscriptural apotelesmatic theory.

William Shea adds additional weight to the case for considering a day to represent a year: "With the description of literal persons, places, and events in classical prophecy one naturally expects literal time units to be employed. With the symbolic figures found in apocalyptic [prophecy], on the other hand, one naturally expects to find symbolic time employed. This leads to the general rule—literal prophecy: literal time—symbolic prophecy: symbolic time." [11]

Shea concludes: "The application of a day for a year in apocalyptic prophecy has been a standard principle of Protestant prophetic interpretation from the time of the Reformation in the 16th century to the 19th century. With the rise of literary criticism of the Bible in the 19th century, the critical school of interpreters abandoned this principle in favor of interpreting these apocalyptic time periods as all having been fulfilled literally in the past, during the days of the Hellenistic kingdoms and the Roman Empire. The majority of Evangelical scholars now apply some of these time prophecies in the future with literal time for a yet future antichrist. . . . At this time in our Church history when our attention has been called to some of the doctrines of the Reformers, such as justification and righteousness by faith, we would do well to heed their principles of prophetic interpretation also." [12]

Could Christ Have Come?

Since Daniel's prophecies obviously extend beyond the early church era, let us investigate the second possibility for resolving our dilemma: Does the New Testament rule out the possibility of a first-century Advent?

Few scholars, if any, would deny that the early Christians did expect Jesus to return in their generation. The question is whether or not this interpretation was authorized by God. Some will allow that the Lord permitted His people to look prematurely for His Son, hiding a delay of nearly two thousand years called for in Daniel's prophecies. This group contends that it would have broken the heart of the early church to learn of the long absence of their beloved Saviour, so Jesus, who had many things to tell them that they could not bear, permitted or even encouraged belief in what was impossible. In other words, Christ fostered a false hope.

A number of New Testament passages clearly confront this theory. The Sanctuary Review Committee[13] acknowledged in their consensus document the "strong and widespread sense of the imminent second advent that we find in the New Testament (e.g., Rom. 13:11, 12; 1 Cor. 7:29-31; Rev. 22:20)." [14]

Each of these several scriptures cited by this committee is quite convincing in proof that a first-century Advent was God's intent. *The Seventh-day Adventist Bible Commentary* furnishes further passages from the book of Revelation and concludes that "the concept of the imminence of the return of Jesus is thus both explicit and implicit throughout the book." [15]

Now both of our first two options have been eliminated—Daniel does project centuries into the Christian era, and the New Testament does provide for an immediate return of Jesus. Is there, then, some way to reconcile Daniel's long-term prophecies with the undeniable New Testament expectancy?

The Key Is Conditional

The answer is found in the conditional nature of prophecy, which we saw applied in the events at the close of the seventy weeks. According to *The SDA Bible Commentary:* "If the [Jewish] nation had been faithful to its trust and had appreciated the high destiny reserved for it by God, the whole earth would have awaited the coming of the Messiah with eager expectancy. He would have come, He would have died, and would have risen again. Jerusalem would have become a great missionary center (*Christ's Object Lessons,* by Ellen G. White, p. 232), and the earth would have been set ablaze with the light of truth in one grand, final appeal to those who had not as yet accepted the invitation of divine mercy." [16]

But the chosen people failed to recognize their potential. So God's plan for the Jews was detoured into the establishment of the Christian church. The church likewise failed to cooperate with God's intenton of a quick consummation. Our commentary continues:

"It seems clear that although the fact of Christ's second coming is not based on any conditions, the repeated statements of Scripture that the coming was imminent were conditional on the response of the church to the challenge of finishing the work of the gospel in their generation. The Word of God, which centuries ago declared that the day of Christ was 'at hand' (Rom. 13:12), has not failed. *Jesus would have come very quickly if the church had done its appointed work. . . .*

"To be sure, God foreknew that the coming of Christ would be delayed some two thousand years, but when He sent messages to the church by the apostles He couched those messages in terms of His will and purpose with regard to that event, in order to make His people conscious of the fact that, *in the divine providence, no delay was necessary.* Consequently, the seven statements of the Revelation concerning the nearness of Christ's coming are to be understood in terms of God's will and purpose, as promises conditionally set forth, and not as utterances based on divine foreknowledge. *In this fact, doubtless, is to be found the harmony between those passages that exhort to readiness for the soon coming of Christ and those time prophecies that reveal how far ahead lay the actual day of the Lord.*" [17]

Foreknowledge Is Fundamental

Another demonstration of God's foreknowledge of man's unfaithfulness even as He expressed His purpose for obedience was seen in the Garden of Eden. "With precious blood, as of a lamb unblemished and spotless," Christ "was foreknown *before* the foundation of the world" (1 Peter 1:19, 20). Even so, "His own purpose and grace which was granted us in Christ Jesus *from all eternity*" (2 Tim. 1:9) was not revealed to Adam and Eve. They were not told they would fall and need a Saviour. God only expressed His plan for them to " 'be fruitful and multiply, and fill the earth'" (Gen. 1:28) as they remained loyal to Him. Likewise, Jesus sent forth His church to "'go into all the world and preach the gospel to all creation'" (Mark 16:15) with the potential of His quick return.

Both of these commissions expressed God's will. Both times His people failed. Both times God's foreknowledge had already ordained a plan to deal with an emergency He knew would happen.

To illustrate this, suppose that a child, warned by his parents to refrain from between-meal forays into the cookie jar, should succumb to temptation anyway. There in the jar he pulls out, along with the forbidden snack, a note offering forgiveness. The fact that the parents foresaw the sin and made prior provision did not rob their child of free will. Even so, when God predicted lives of evil, as with Esau, Pharaoh, and Judas, His prophecy was not responsible for their rebellion. He foresaw their evil attitudes and exposed them beforehand, making sure to set limits upon their ability to harm and hurt. He foreknows and restrains evil nations, as well as individuals (see Dan. 2:21; 4:17). His prior announcements of their existence and activities demonstrates, first of all, that He is never caught by surprise. His announced foreknowledge also proves His sovereign control over the universe, to cause "all things to work together for good" for those who choose to love Him and accept His gracious purposes. This brings Him glory.[18]

Definite Hints

Although the New Testament constantly advertises the inevitability of Christ's soon advent, it gives definite hints that the blessed event would suffer delay. Immediately following His prediction of those last-day events that would precede and accompany His return, Jesus in the parable of the ten virgins foretold the delay of the bridegroom's coming, during which they all became weary of waiting (Matt. 25:5). Right after this parable He revealed in another one that "'*after a long time* the master . . . came and settled accounts'" (verse 19). In this same context Christ warned about the evil slave who concluded, "'"My master is not coming for a long time"'" (chap. 24:48). Paul too instructed the Thessalonians not to expect Christ immediately: He "will not come unless the apostasy comes first, and the man of lawlessness is revealed" (2 Thess. 2:3). Finally, the book of Revelation amplifies this prediction of the antichrist by repeating the 1,260-year prophecy of Daniel 7. So amid all the enthusiasm for the Saviour's soon return are also indications that God's purpose would suffer delay before finally meeting fulfillment long centuries later.

No More Gymnastics

In summary, we have seen the apparent contradiction between the immediate expectancy of the early Christians and the ages to come required by Daniel's prophecies resolved in the conditional nature of those prophecies that involve human cooperation. God's foreknowledge has emergency plans prepared for man's disobedience even as He announces His will for us to obey.

Having solved this perplexity, we can acknowledge the obvious potential for the return of Christ in the age of the apostles. And we need not perform Biblical gymnastics by trying to force all of Daniel's prophecies into a first-century fulfillment.

The Adventist sanctuary doctrine has proved to be solid Biblical truth. And we have seen that the pre-Advent judgment, when properly understood, enhances rather than obstructs one's assurance of salvation. Now that that prophetic position is found to be firmly established throughout the Old Testament, we may face with confidence the questions that confront us in the New.

11 Clean Before the Lord

nticipation electrifies the air each autumn as millions of American sportsaholics welcome their World Series. All teams but two have fallen along with the early October leaves. Finally the survivors face off in baseball's annual championship.

The 1965 classic, which matched the Los Angeles Dodgers with the Minnesota Twins, promised excitement aplenty. Could Sandy Koufax, fireball ace of the Dodgers, silence the booming bats of the American League champs? Everyone waited for October 6, the opening day of the series.

But that Wednesday afternoon as the players lined up before their cheering worshipers, someone was missing. Someone significant. Where was Koufax?

You would have to ask Moses. You see, by God's instruction Moses had enjoined upon the Jews seven sacred sabbaths to be remembered each year. Yom Kippur, the Day of Atonement, was the most solemn of all. In 1965 this holy day coincided with the opening game of the series. Koufax, being Jewish, had driven past the ballpark to the synagogue.

Why is Yom Kippur so important that Koufax would miss his most important baseball assignment of the year? Let us visit the Old Testament tabernacle to trace the holy day's roots.

Twice each day throughout the year the Hebrew priests sacrificed innocent substitutes at the sanctuary for the sins of the camp. Finally came the Day of Atonement, when those who accepted God's terms of salvation were separated from those who refused Him. It was the annual execution of judgment.

A quaint bit of Jewish heritage, one would imagine. With no relevance to New Testament Christians, right? After all, how could freedom in Christ relate to this ancient ritual of the old covenant?

A Relevant Ritual

Adventists have always taught otherwise. Since its inception the church has insisted that Jesus' work begun in 1844 was a part of the antitype of the Day of Atonement. As might be expected, this pillar of faith has been repulsed from outside the church and hotly disputed within. Should the pioneers' concept of end-time atonement be retired with their horses and buggies? Does the science of

Biblical scholarship expose it as a useless relic? How did Adventists reach their unique concept of atonement?

The pioneers blazed an interesting trail. First they learned in the Millerite movement that the sanctuary would be "cleansed" (Dan. 8:14, K.J.V.). After their interpretation was dashed in the great Disappointment, a remnant restudied the subject. They moved in their study to Leviticus 16 and related the cleansing of the sanctuary on the Day of Atonement to Daniel 8. Were they right in joining the two passages? Is there a legitimate connection between them? A crucial question indeed, which we will confront in this chapter on atonement.

Here is our problem: Although the King James Version offers "cleanse" or "cleansed" in both places, the original language uses separate words that do not quite match. According to the General Conference Glacier View consensus document, in Daniel 8 "its basic idea is to 'make right,' 'justify,' 'vindicate,' or 'restore'; but 'purify' and 'cleanse' may be included within its conceptual range. In Daniel 8:14 it is evident that the word denotes the reversal of the evil caused by the power symbolized by the 'little horn' [K.J.V.], and hence probably should be translated 'restore.' "[1] The document then acknowledges that "there is, therefore, not a strong verbal link between this verse and the Day of Atonement ritual of Leviticus 16."[2] Can we build strong doctrine upon a weak foundation? Must we then disqualify an 1844 Day of Atonement?

Certainly not. Another bond, strong and undeniable, connects Daniel and Leviticus. "The passages are, nevertheless, related by their parallel ideas of rectifying the sanctuary from the effects of sin."[3] More on this later. There is even a convincing verbal link between Leviticus and Daniel: "It is a striking fact that the term qodesh, meaning 'sanctuary' in Daniel 8:14, is the very term used seven times in Leviticus 16 (2, 3, 16, 17, 20, 23, 27) with the meaning of 'sanctuary' or 'Holy of Holies.' Thus this key term within the context of the cleansing of the sanctuary in Leviticus 16 appears in Daniel 8:14."[4]

The link between Daniel and Leviticus is clear. As we now examine the meaning of the Day of Atonement, this connection becomes compelling.

But wait. Was not atonement made at the cross, ages before 1844? One goal of the 490 years in Daniel 9 was " 'to make atonement for iniquity' " (verse 24). We Adventists insist that all six goals in verse 24 needed to be completed by A.D. 34. Since atonement was accomplished at the cross, how, then, could the Day of Atonement not begin until 1844?

Here is an objection to Adventism that requires response. When does atonement take place? First we must know its meaning.

Atonement means to "cover over, pacify, propitiate [provide satisfaction for sin]."[5] Its root is "to cover."[6] This basic form is seen in Genesis 6:14, when Noah was instructed to make an ark and " 'cover it' " with pitch. Out of the simple definition of covering come the derived meanings of appeasement and making matters right, as seen in Jacob's attempt to " 'appease' " the offended Esau with gifts (chap. 32:20). An illustration of both covering and conciliation is the use of the word as " 'mercy seat' " in Exodus 25:17. Mercy covers, or shields, the sinner from justice, and also makes satisfaction for its claims. "Atonement is God's way of bringing about a reconciliation, of winning man back to Himself. Hence the English word 'at-one-ment.' " [7]

Although examples abound in Scripture, most Christians have a limited concept of atonement. More than forgiveness through a substitute's sacrifice is involved. Punishment of the guilty is considered atonement too. When an Israelite leader brought a Midianite prostitute into his tent, Phinehas, grandson of Aaron the high priest, took a spear and killed them both. The Bible says Phinehas " " "made atonement for the sons of Israel" ' " (Num. 25:13) by punishing the sinner for his crime. Divine justice was conciliated by the death of the guilty. A similar example is the " 'atonement' " made for the murder of the Gibeonites (2 Sam. 2:1-3). The stoning of greedy Achan is another exhibit of divine disfavor being expiated by the execution of the evildoer. Evidently all punishment, whether by substitution or direct visitation, is considered atonement. Everything leading to a solution to the sin problem is included, not just forgiveness.

Atonement was accomplished in three phases: (1) consecration of the sanctuary system, (2) the covering of sin, and (3) cleansing the sanctuary. Let us learn more about each function.

Inaugural Atonement

First there was a seven-day inauguration for the sanctuary system. This was for Aaron and his sons to " 'anoint them and ordain them and consecrate them, that they may serve Me as priests' " (Ex. 28:41). " 'Atonement was made at their ordination and consecration' " (chap. 29:33).

This start-up ceremony also dedicated the building itself for service. " 'For seven days you shall make atonement for the altar and consecrate it,' " (verse 37). Even the Most Holy Place was entered for this atonement, in an anointing ceremony (chap. 30:26).

Continual Atonement

Following the installment of the sanctuary and its priests, the daily service began covering the sins of repenting believers. Every morning and evening a substitute was sacrificed for the sins of everyone (chap. 29:38-42). But this provision did not bring forgiveness unless personally accepted. The penitent sinner brought his substitute to the tabernacle. Then he would " ' "lay his hand on the head of the sin offering, and slay the sin offering at the place of the burnt offering. And the priest shall take some of its blood with his finger and put it on the horns of the altar of burnt offering; and all the rest of its blood he shall pour out at the base of the altar. . . . Thus the priest shall make atonement for him, and he shall be forgiven" ' " (Lev. 4:29-31).

So this process of everyday forgiveness was also considered atonement. [8] The twice-daily sacrifices, representing Calvary, *provided* atonement, and individual guilt offerings *appropriated* atonement. Both were necessary for sin to be covered.

Atonement in the daily service brought complete freedom from guilt. Notice: " 'Now if a person sins . . . , he *is* guilty and shall bear his punishment. He is then to bring to the priest a ram without defect . . . for a guilt offering. So the priest shall make atonement for him . . . , and it shall be forgiven him. It is a guilt offering; he *was* certainly guilty before the Lord' " (chap. 5:17-19).

See the sequence? Man sins. He *is* guilty and due for punishment. But a substitute suffers that doom. Atonement is made. He *was* guilty and now is free. How free? Free as a bird loosed from captivity, according to one ceremony of the daily service" (chap. 14:1-7).

This freedom from guilt was *unreserved but not unconditional.* There was no "once saved, always saved" back then, either. Remember the parable? The servant is forgiven his huge debt but refuses to show the same mercy to another. Forgiveness is canceled. He goes into prison until he shall " 'repay all that was owed' " (Matt. 18:34). *He had been freely forgiven, but when he stepped back outside of mercy he was again held guilty for sins previously covered.* His only safety was continual atonement.

Everyday atonement is a major theme of Leviticus. And the Day of Atonement was not the only holy day on which atonement was made. On Pentecost, for example, a goat was offered for atonement (Num. 28:30). Then why have a separate Day of Atonement?

Cleansing Atonement

Consider the operation of a corporation. In their offices, executives continually hold informal conferences as a necessary function of business. Yet there remains a special conference room where scheduled, systematic meetings make official, final decisions touching the universal range of business matters.

Likewise with the Day of Atonement. Atonement continued throughout the year as a necessary function of salvation. Yet a special time and place was reserved for a systematic, final ceremony to settle the universal aspects of atonement.

This Day of Atonement, the climax of all religious activity, was a solemn time of judgment—investigation, vindication, and punishment. How was all this accomplished?

The whole camp was summoned to set aside its work and gather together around the tabernacle. Next there was a judgment between rival systems, symbolized by lots cast between goats. The blood of the winner was brought inside to cleanse the sanctuary. After sprinkling this blood throughout the building the priest emerged to bless the waiting people. Those who refused to participate in atonement were cut off from the camp. The losing goat was banished to the wilderness.

What did this ceremony represent? First, the government of our God, who saves sinners by His sacrifice, was vindicated. As His defeated rival was set aside, the sanctuary—His system of salvation—was authorized to accept blood for its cleansing. Inside the most holy apartment his sacred law was vindicated—blood was sprinkled to satisfy its claims. In this the high priest made " 'atonement for the holy place, because of the impurities of the sons of Israel' " (Lev. 16:16). How had the sins of God's children defiled His sanctuary?

In daily atonement, the penitent confessed guilt on the head of the substitute to be slain. After the blood was applied to the altar, the sinner was free. What had happened? God took the blame upon Himself. Each day's atonement transferred more and more sin to His account in the sanctuary. Then once each year the Lord released Himself of this accumulating burden of responsibility. Atoning blood was brought into the sanctuary, and also was sprinkled on the horns of the altar to " 'cleanse it, and from the impurities of the sons of Israel consecrate it' " (verse 19). Now the believers' sins that had been forgiven and covered by God were symbolically blotted out of record. " 'Atonement shall be made for you to cleanse you; you shall be clean from all your sins before the Lord' " (verse 30).

We should note that blood did not symbolically pollute the sanctuary. As a symbol, blood covered and cleansed. Sin defiled. Sins were recorded on the heavenly books when committed, not when they were confessed. Atoning blood removed guilt from the confessor by symbolically covering sins already recorded.

Now we must face the question Why not have an immediate blotting out with forgiveness? Why the middle phase of covering sin until final cleansing on the Day of Atonement?

Recall that atonement comprises the total scope of dealing with the sin problem—not just the daily covering of guilt. Its ultimate goal is to restore oneness with God by entirely eradicating sin from the universe. This requires expiation, or punishment. In the Jewish sanctuary, sins could be covered by daily atonement only because the substitute had been punished. And those sins not confessed and covered by the blood were due for later reckoning. This execution of doom, being necessary in blotting out sin, was also considered atonement. Therefore a final Day of Atonement was needed to execute judgment—vindication and restoration as well as punishment.

Satan, the inventor and salesman of sin, must be dealt with in final atonement. Sin, after all, is a partnership affair. Certainly a high school dope addict is liable under law, but so is the drug pusher. Even more so. So simple justice demands that the devil be punished for instigating sin, even though an innocent Substitute already has suffered for the sins of the tempter's prey.

Remember the two goats? While the Lord's goat made atonement for believers, the rival was regarded as responsible for all wickedness. Its proper name in the original is Azazel, a powerful spirit or demon. Since early Christian times Azazel has been recognized as a symbol for Satan.[9] According to Leviticus 16:10, the priest also made " 'atonement upon it [Azazel], to send it into the wilderness.' "

This, of course, was a different type of atonement. It was not redemptive—no blood was shed. Christ was not punished for the devil's sins. Satan must suffer for his own.

So must his followers. After atonement was completed in the Most Holy Place, the priest emerged to execute the verdict. Because unbelievers had refused God's provision for atonement, they faced their own punishment: " 'If there is any person who will not humble himself on this same day, he shall be cut off from his people' " (chap. 23:29).

Those who had gathered around the sanctuary to trust the blood of atonement were pronounced clean before God. In a few days the harvest celebration of the Feast of Tabernacles began.

So the Day of Atonement fulfilled its goal of closing the book on sin. The God of the sanctuary was vindicated in His government of grace. Those who had been covered were now cleansed and pronounced fit for the harvest celebration. All who refused atonement were cut of. Azazel was banished. Everything was finally settled—atonement was complete. The camp was clean.

Atonement Now

The continuing importance of atonement today should be obvious. Yes, Christ on the cross did " 'make atonement for iniquity,' " as Daniel had foretold. Sins are completely paid for! Yet the same verse also promised He would " 'anoint the most holy place' " (Dan. 9:24). Only then could He continue the atoning process of covering confessing believers as our heavenly high priest. Finally He completes atonement by cleansing the sanctuary and the universe with that all-sufficient atoning sacrifice He made on the cross.

Meanwhile, our sins are forgiven and we are free! This freedom from guilt, while unreserved, requires that we abide in Christ—there is no once saved, always saved.

The year 1844 introduced the final, cleansing phase of atonement. This cleansing, or blotting out of sins, must precede the refreshing of God's Spirit that heralds the coming of Christ and the final restoration: " 'Repent therefore and return, that your sins may be wiped away, *in order that* times of refreshing may come from the presence of the Lord; and that He may send Jesus, the Christ appointed for you, whom heaven must receive until the period of restoration of all things' " (Acts 3:19-21).

Christ had foretold that " 'he who overcomes shall thus be clothed in white garments; and I will not erase his name from the book of life, and I will confess his name before My Father, and before His angels' " (Rev. 3:5). " 'Everyone therefore who shall confess Me before men, I will also confess him before My Father who is in heaven. But whoever shall deny Me before men, I will also deny him before My Father who is in heaven' " (Matt. 10:32, 33).

Our choice is simple. Either our sins or our name will be blotted out. If we confess Christ—trusting in His overcoming blood while obeying His command-ments—our *sins* will be removed from the books of record. But if we reject or neglect His salvation, our *name* will be erased from the Lamb's book of life.

Just as Azazel was banished from the camp, when Christ emerges from the heavenly sanctuary to bless His waiting people the devil is exiled to the wilderness of the abyss. Following this, "then comes the end, when He [Christ] delivers up the kingdom to the God and Father, when He has abolished all rule and all authority and power. For He must reign until He has put all His enemies under His feet. The last enemy that will be abolished is death. . . . And when all things are subjected to Him, then the Son Himself also will be subjected to the One who subjected all things to Him, that God may be all in all" (1 Cor. 15:24-28).

Atonement is complete. "The great controversy is ended. Sin and sinners are no more. The entire universe is clean. One pulse of harmony and gladness beats through the vast creation." [10] No more doubt in any mind—God is love!

Why Worry?

Fellow Christians often insist that the Adventist belief in a future blotting out of sins must leave a person unsure about eternal life. Why? With the assurance of sins forgiven, nobody worries about getting to heaven. So why be anxious about the cleansing of the sanctuary? Both the trip to heaven and the blotting out of sins are promised by God. Neither has happened yet. In Christ we are assured of both. Meanwhile our sins are covered and we are free. The problem, you see, is not the concept of atonement, but the baggage of fear some have brought into this beautiful Christian doctrine.

Atonement, then, is a continuous process of forgiveness completed by a "graduation" ceremony that cleanses the sanctuary. "On the positive side atonement includes the restoration of oneness and harmony throughout the universe. On the negative side atonement is the elimination of sin to the satisfaction of the moral universe." [11]

The pioneers correctly taught that the ancient day of judgment prefigured the closing events of the cosmic great controversy. This truth of end-time atonement rings loud and clear for all who have ears to hear.

Something else rings true—gospel liberty. The same freedom of forgiveness that sparkles throughout the New Testament is found in this Old Testament ceremony.

The Old, Old Story

Human works were illegal on judgment day: " 'Neither shall you do any work on this same day, for it is a day of atonement, to make atonement *on your behalf* before the Lord your God' " (Lev. 23:28). All hope was focused outside believers in the atonement made *for* them. Whoever rejected the blood by indulging in works qualified for wrath. God was serious: " 'As for any person who does any work on this same day, that person I will destroy from among his people. You shall do *no work* at all' " (verses 30, 31). What a beautiful picture of the gospel! Who can say that Adventist doctrine is legalistic?

On this day of judgment extra incense was offered, symbolizing total dependence upon the merits of Jesus. How humbling for human pride—the only thing that counted was the blood: " 'Atonement shall be made *for you* to cleanse you; you shall be clean from all your sins before the Lord' " (chap. 16:30). The saints were clean before the Lord because of the blood shed *for* them, not because of infallible sanctification attained *within.* They were not asked to present fruit God had grown with their cooperation. Nor were they allowed to wave palm branches of personal testimony. Instead, they were required to be silent and empty-handed, for their only salvation was the blood. Judgment was based entirely on their willingness to come apart from the world, lay aside their works, and trust in the atonement made for them. If their behavior demonstrated that they did indeed obey God's terms of salvation, no further investigation was made. " 'He who believes in Him is not judged' " (John 3:18). " 'The blood shall be to you for a token upon the houses where ye are: and when I see the blood I will pass over you' " (Ex. 12:13).

Certainly all sincere believers experienced spiritual growth. God's law was evident in their lives. But they could not approach God on the basis of their sanctification, since all "fall short of the glory of God" (Rom. 3:23). Those who obeyed God's terms of atonement were not in jeopardy regarding their shortfall of personal righteousness. They had assurance of acceptance through their substitute.

The Caring Church

The Day of Atonement provides essential insight into the practical nature of Heaven's holy law. Believers united with God's family around the sanctuary. We today comprise one body with Christ as head. Growing up into Jesus, therefore, means growing closer to one another. This eliminates the monastery mentality of "holy loners" in solitary striving for the goal of personal purity. *Private victory over sin, while an essential fruit of the gospel, is not an end in itself.* Overcoming sin means removing obstacles that prevent expression of love to God and neighbor—fulfillment of the law. For example, we must shun impure thoughts. Why? To preserve the family circle. Also, to respect others as children of God, brothers and sisters, not mistreating them as objects of lust. And why do we avoid overeating? To feed the hungry and have a long, healthy life for glorifying God in service to society. The present emphasis in the North American Division on the Caring Church is a divinely inspired attempt to revive the primitive godliness we have missed since the days of Pentecost. At that time, you recall, all were together in one accord. This unity is the substance of the last six commandments and the proof of the first four. It is the latter-rain experience of the remnant "who keep the commandments of God and their faith in Jesus" (Rev. 14:12).

A Compelling Connection

Now at the close of this chapter on atonement, we can fully appreciate the compelling connection between Daniel 8 and Leviticus 16:

Daniel 8

1. *God's rulership is vindicated* as His government of grace in the sanctuary defeats the challenge of the little horn.

2. *Satan's challenge is defeated* as his earthly agent, the little horn, is turned back from defiling the sanctuary.

3. *The saints are vindicated* as the sanctuary system, through which they receive forgiveness, is upheld against the little horn.

Leviticus 16

1. *God's rulership is vindicated* as His sacrifice is judged worthy to atone for sin. His sanctuary system of forgiving guilt through the blood is upheld as the sins it covered all year are now blotted out.

2. *Satan's challenge is defeated.* The originator of sin is pronounced guilty and is banished from society. Those who join his rebellion by refusing to believe in the blood are cut off.

3. *The saints are vindicated.* Their participation in the sanctuary system is evident, and they are vindicated with it. All along they have been forgiven in the blood. Now their sins, which had been covered, are blotted out.

Smoothly Flowing River

In this investigation of end-time atonement, another pillar of Adventist pioneers stands vindicated. There is indeed a smoothy flowing river connecting Daniel with Leviticus. A river of atoning blood to wash away the sin of a guilty world. What a wonderful treasury of truth we have to share!

12 When Freedom Reigns

Don't bother me with your beasts!" chided an "evangelical" Adventist from California. As her tanned face turned the color of the great red dragon she continued, "I'm through with Revelation and its scary symbols. What we need is the gospel—Christ and Him crucified! That's all!"

Amen? Many agree that magnifying the cross minimizes doctrine. Especially prophecy. Robert Brinsmead quotes the famous evangelist Spurgeon:

" 'More and more I am jealous lest any views upon prophecy, church government, politics, or even systematic theology, should withdraw one of us from glorifying in the Cross of Christ. Salvation is a theme for which I would fain enlist every holy tongue. I am greedy after witnesses for the glorious Gospel of the blessed God. O that Christ crucified were the universal burden of men of God. Your guess at the number of the beast, . . . your conjectures concerning a personal antichrist—forgive me, I count them but mere bones for dogs; while men are dying and hell is filling, it seems to me the veriest drivel to be muttering about an Armageddon.' " [1]

Preach the crucified Christ! Good advice, indeed. Nothing else can bring peace to troubled hearts. Without doubt, the beasts and dragons of Revelation are awesome, even fearsome. No wonder the book is a breeding ground for fearmongers who have no appreciation for grace or solid Christian doctrine. Unfortunately, even the Adventist Church has sometimes preached the beast and its mark more than the Lamb and His blood, and symbols more than the Saviour. [2] Should the prophetic instruction be ignored, then, because of this abuse? Does Calvary destroy or depreciate that third of the Bible that is composed of prophecy? Or could the cross rather enhance our appreciation for predictions of the end of the world?

Bones for Dogs?

What is prophecy, anyway? "Bones for dogs"? God forbid. The same Jesus who died for our sins is coming again! This is the point of the Patmos revelation, its purpose and message. A brief tour of the final book of the Bible will document this.

Its first five words set the theme for what follows: "The revelation of Jesus Christ." Although earthly prophetic beasts are mentioned thirty-seven times in its twenty-two chapters, Jesus is the center of attention. Even the "beast chapter," Revelation 13, tells of "the Lamb who has been slain" (verse 8). A touching gem of the gospel follows the introduction and opens the door to the rest of the book: "To Him who loves us, and released us from our sins by His blood" (chap. 1:5).

After a majestic description of the glorified Jesus, Revelation proceeds with seven love letters to the churches—"tough love" for those who had fallen from their first love. Because of the trouble the churches were soon to suffer, their Shepherd urges them to " ' "be faithful until death, and I will give you the crown of life" ' " (chap. 2:10). " ' "Hold fast until I come" ' " (verse 25).

His dire warnings are tempered with tenderness, even in the Laodicean message. Adventists recognize the relevance of this radical rebuke to lukewarm lovers: " ' "So because you are lukewarm, and neither hot nor cold, I will spit you out of My mouth" ' " (chap. 3:16).[3]

I used to cringe at the thought of being spit out. It seemed crude, even cruel. Then one day I noticed that the margin of my Bible read "vomit." Curious, I did a word study. Yes, indeed, the marginal reading was supported. Lukewarm love makes Christ ill. Though morally above reproach, our hearts are too callous to appreciate His marvelous love. We do not smoke, but neither are we on fire. We do not drink, but we refuse to be under His influence. We do not dance, but neither do we delight in His salvation. This naughty neutrality nauseates Him, and He is about to vomit our phony devotion. An awful thought indeed. But this is involuntary expulsion, not disgusted rejection. While this certainly is not a pretty picture, we find comfort in knowing that Christ does not want to repel us. This severe letter closes with a heart-touching invitation to His lukewarm lovers and a glorious promise for eternity: " ' "Behold, I stand at the door and knock; if anyone hears My voice and opens the door, I will come in to him, and will dine with him, and he with Me. He who overcomes, I will grant to him to sit down with Me on My throne, as I also overcame and sat down with My Father on His throne" ' " (verses 20, 21).

What precious manna from heaven! Dogs must go elsewhere for their bones.

Striking Similarity

Immediately following the letter to Laodicea comes the only picture of the pre-Advent judgment scene in the New Testament, a passage parallel, in fact, with Daniel 7. Notice the striking similarity between these twin prophecies:

DANIEL 7		REVELATION 4 AND 5
7:9	Thrones set	4:2
7:9	God on the throne	4:2
7:9, 10	Description of scene	4:3-6
7:10	Myriads of angels	5:11

7:10	Books	5:2-9
7:10	Opening of books	5:2-9
7:13	Jesus in humanity	5:5
7:13	Jesus comes before throne	5:7
7:14	Christ receives kingdom	5:12, 13
7:22	Saints favorably accepted	5:9
7:22	Saints receive kingdom	5:10

Among these parallels, some are especially notable. Daniel 7:10 and Revelation 5:11 are the only places in the Bible that number the angels in this particular way. In fact, *The New International Version* gives identical wording. Also, the opening of books is symbolic of judgment (cf. Dan. 7:10 with Rev. 20:11, 12). Both times Christ is presented as a member of the human family (remember that the humanity of Jesus qualifies Him to defend us in our judgment—recall John 5:26, 27). In both passages the books are opened—evidently Jesus devotes a phase of His priestly ministry to judgment.

The connection between Daniel 7 and Revelation 4 and 5 is cemented as we notice those three elements of judgment identical in both passages:

Daniel 7

1. *God's rulership is vindicated* as Christ is " 'given dominion, glory and a kingdom' " (verse 14).

2. *Satan's challenge is defeated,* for dominion is awarded to the Son of man.

3. *The saints are vindicated,* for they take "possession of the kingdom" (verse 22).

Revelation 4 and 5

1. *God's rulership is vindicated* as Christ is accorded " 'glory and dominion.' " " 'Worthy is the Lamb that was slain to receive power . . . and glory' " (chap. 5:13, 12).

2. *Satan's challenge is defeated,* for dominion is awarded to the Lamb.

3. *The saints are vindicated,* for the verdict of this judgment " 'made them to be a kingdom . . . ; and they will reign upon the earth' " (verse 10).

Historic Adventism Vindicated

Beyond question, this particular judgment did not happen at the cross. Notice the careful distinction between the timing of redemption and judgment. Redemption is *past;* judgment is *present:* "And they sang a new song, saying, 'Worthy art Thou to take the book [present], and to break its seals [present]; for thou wast slain [past], and didst purchase for God with Thy blood [past] men from every tribe' " (verse 9). " 'The Lion that is from the tribe of Judah, the Root of

David, has overcome [past] so as to open the book [present]'" (verse 5).

This clear separation between redemption accomplished at the cross and the future time when Christ comes to the Father to open the book of judgment definitely supports the doctrine of pre-Advent judgment. Here we have vital New Testament vindication of historic Adventism.

The judgment scene of Revelation 4 and 5 is the cornerstone of the book. Everything that precedes builds up to this event. The first chapter establishes Christ's credentials as true Lord of this world in celestial majesty; the next two chapters prepare the churches for the judgment of chapters 4 and 5. Everything that follows refers to and revolves around this court of the great cosmic controversy. A review of the final chapters makes this evident.

Freedom Reigns

First, God wins endorsement for His freedom to reign: "The seventh angel sounded; and there arose loud voices in heaven, saying, 'The kingdom of the world has become the kingdom of our Lord, and of His Christ; and He will reign forever and ever'" (chap. 11:15).[4] After His sanctuary has been vindicated in the judgment of Revelation 4 and 5, God executes the verdict: "'We give Thee thanks . . . because Thou hast taken Thy great power and hast begun to reign'" (verse 17). The time has come for "'wrath'" and "'reward'" (verse 18): "And the temple of God which is in heaven was opened, and the ark of His covenant appeared in His temple, and there were flashes of lightning and sounds and peals of thunder and an earthquake and a great hailstorm" (verse 19).

The saints share their Lord's victory: "And I heard a loud voice in heaven, saying, 'Now the salvation, and the power, and the kingdom of our God and the authority of His Christ have come, for the accuser of our brethren has been thrown down, who accuses them before our God day and night. And they overcame him because of the blood of the Lamb and because of the word of their testimony, and they did not love their life even to death'" (chap. 12:10, 11). "'Rejoice over her [Babylon], O heaven, and you saints and apostles and prophets, because God has pronounced judgment *for* you *against* her'" (chap. 18:20).

Next, the seven last plagues come from "out of the temple" (chap. 15:6) upon the wicked. These punishments are terrible, but the universe is convinced that "'they deserve it'" (chap. 16:6). "'Yes, O Lord God, the Almighty, true and righteous are Thy judgments'" (verse 7).

Finally, "a loud voice came out of the temple from the throne, saying, 'It is done'" (verse 17). *All these climactic acts of the great controversy come from the sanctuary after God has been vindicated in the judgment.*

This judgment weds Christ to His church: "'Hallelujah! For the Lord our God, the Almighty, reigns. Let us rejoice and be glad and give the glory to Him, for the marriage of the Lamb has come and His bride has made herself ready'" (chap. 19:6, 7). Christ's family has been sealed to Him, and He has been sealed to them. Finally He can come to take them home. "And I saw heaven opened; and behold, a white horse, and He who sat upon it is called Faithful and True; and in righteousness He judges and wages war" (verse 11). The wicked are slain, and the devil, like the scapegoat on the ancient Day of Atonement, is exiled. God's people are transported " ' "to the marriage supper of the Lamb" ' " (verse 9).

In Revelation 14 we see the results of the judgment proclaimed:

1. *God is vindicated* by the message to " 'fear God, and give Him glory, because the hour of His judgment has come; and worship Him' " (verse 7).

2. *Satan's challenge is defeated* by the verdict against Babylon, his agent that adulterated the sanctuary truth (verse 8). Disciples of the devil are rewarded with the mark of the beast. From "out of the temple" they are reaped in the ripe harvest of wrath (verses 15-19).

3. *The saints are vindicated.* Those "who keep the commandments of God and their faith in Jesus" (verse 12) through the crisis are favored by judgment: " ' "Blessed are the dead who die in the Lord from now on!" ' " (verse 13).

In summary, Christ won " 'the keys of death and of Hades' " (chap. 1:18) at the cross, but not until later does He use those keys to open the book of judgment. God is vindicated as worthy of worship, Satan's counterfeit is defeated, and the saints overcome in the blood of the Lamb. Clearly, the Adventist doctrine of pre-Advent judgment rests on solid ground throughout Revelation.[5]

Heartwarming Assurance

Now let us enjoy the heartwarming assurance our loving Father has given us in Revelation 5. The central question of the judgment is Who is worthy? Who "deserves and is morally fit" (verse 2, Amplified) to participate in judgment? The Patmos prophet expectantly waits for someone to step forward. Perhaps Elijah? No. Maybe Moses? No. Surely Enoch, who walked with God! But "no one in heaven [not Enoch], or on the earth [not even the 144,000], or under the earth [including the apostle Paul in his grave], was able" (verse 3) to take part in the judgment. Even Enoch, like everyone else, needed a Substitute.

Now the prophet "began to weep greatly, because no one was found worthy" (verse 4). What hope did he have to pass the judgment if Enoch could not participate? Finally, in a most dramatic scene, Jesus is presented: " 'Do not weep! See, the Lion of the tribe of Judah, the Root of David, has triumphed. He is able to open the scroll and its seven seals' " (verse 5, N.I.V.). John now sees "a Lamb standing, as if slain," "in the middle of the throne" (verse 6, margin). The sacrifice of Christ is the center of attention. What a lesson! Only the atoning blood of Jesus counts in the judgment. The blood supremely vindicates God.

Only Christ is worthy. Human righteousness is junk in the judgment. Honor and glory belong to Jesus alone. Without our request, permission, or knowledge He provided Himself as the Lamb to satisfy His own infinite claims of law. Now justice joins mercy in calling for the pardon and homecoming of the repenting, trusting sinner.

" ' "Everything is ready; come" ' " (Matt. 22:4, N.E.B.).

13 A Veiled Threat

E ver since the first morning of Seventh-day Adventism as a movement, a veiled threat has hung over the church. Long before the pioneers organized as a denomination or even knew about the Sabbath, this veiled threat challenged their claim to have God's prophetic antidote for the wine of drunken Babylon. And it is still around today.

What is this awesome threat? We must go back to the morning after the great disappointment of 1844. Hiram Edson, you recall, rose from his knees, dried his bitter tears, and left the barn to shore up the spirits of his sorrowing brethren. While crossing a cornfield to avoid the taunts of neighbors, he was met by the message that made the movement: Jesus in 1844 entered "within the veil" (Heb. 6:19) separating the two apartments of the heavenly sanctuary to begin final atonement in the presence of His Father.

Ever since Edson announced his revelation, critics have charged that this veil, which Adventists say Christ passed through in 1844, is a threat to Adventist theology. "Christ went directly through to His Father at His ascension," they insist. "Years later Stephen saw ' "the heavens opened up and the Son of Man standing at the right hand of God" ' (Acts 7:56)—not separated by a veil from His Father for eighteen long centuries. The New Testament says nothing about apartments at God's throne. So there is no two-phase priesthood for Christ. No 1844 atonement. And no need for your church!"

These statements may seem unsettling at first. But when we understand the background and purpose of Hebrews, the veiled threat vanishes. We find the Epistle to be quite a comfortable home for a proper understanding of the two-part priesthood of Jesus.

Purpose Behind the Epistle

What is the story behind Hebrews? The name of the book itself is revealing. Hebrews was written to first-century Christians of Jewish background some thirty years after Christ ascended. It is a letter of pastoral concern and doctrinal instruction.

Why concern? Christianity has always been a challenge for converts from Judaism. Especially, reminded the apostle, in "the former days, when, after being enlightened, you endured a great conflict of sufferings" (chap. 10:32). Now they were starting to backslide. "Please," begged the apostle, " 'do not throw away your confidence' [verse 35]. Let us not be 'of those who shrink back to destruction' [verse 39]. Instead, 'let us draw near' [verse 22], 'let us hold fast the confession of our hope without wavering [verse 23].' "

Constantly throughout the book the Hebrew Christians are exhorted to draw near to God through Jesus. Why? With the return of their Redeemer delayed past expectation, they were tempted to retreat to the rituals of their former religion. They needed explicit instruction in the doctrine of Christ as the divine replacement for the Jewish ceremonial system. Let us hear from its own pages the primary purpose of the book:

"Now the main point in what has been said is this: we have such a high priest, who has taken His seat at the right hand of the throne of the Majesty in the heavens, a minister in the sanctuary, and in the true tabernacle, which the Lord pitched, not man. For every high priest is appointed to offer both gifts and sacrifices; hence it is necessary that this high priest also have something to offer" (chap. 8:1-3).

So Hebrews was programmed to prove that (1) we have a *new High Priest* who ministers for us (2) in a *"new" tabernacle in heaven,* with (3) *something to offer*—"eternal redemption" "through His own blood" (chap. 9:12).

Framed by a Carpenter?

These three facts, so familiar to Adventists today, seemed revolutionary and even sacrilegious in the first century. How could an obscure, unlearned carpenter supplant the system that God Himself had set up and operated personally for thousands of years? A system that the Jews believed would endure for all their generations? Who was this young upstart from the hillbilly province of Galilee who twice chased the priests out of the Temple? Were His followers now trying to do the same thing again with this new heresy about His priesthood?

We can easily see why the dominant theme of Hebrews would have to be the establishment of the all-sufficiency of Calvary's blood, brought into the new heavenly temple by the new High Priest, and the good news that we may have continual access to the Almighty through that precious blood.

Hebrews, then, was written to preserve the first-century Jewish converts by proving that Christ was the fulfillment of their sanctuary system. The author's "purpose was neither to teach nor to deny the two-partite ministry of Christ in the heavenly sanctuary nor to address himself to the chronological aspects of this ministry. . . . One should keep in mind that a book of Scripture does not address itself to every dimension of salvation."[1]

Hebrews Is Not an Island

God does not find it necessary to repeat each aspect of a doctrine at every mention of it in Scripture. For example, the book of James discusses justification (forgiveness), but it was not intended to be a systematic explanation of the doctrine. For a complete view on justification one has to go outside of James to Romans and Galatians. And for a total picture of the sanctuary, one must go outside of Hebrews to Revelation and Daniel. Should we reject what Paul teaches about justification because we would rather hear it all from James? Then why reject the two-phase function of the heavenly sanctuary because it is not outlined in Hebrews as we may wish?

We must remember that the dual ministry of the priesthood, just like the seventh-day Sabbath, was a familiar part of the Hebrew heritage. The author of Hebrews did not waste space needlessly convincing them of these truths. Instead, he focused upon Christ as their center, thereby giving meaning to both already-established doctrines. Those who cannot accept the dual nature of Christ's priesthood because its chronology is not systematically outlined in Hebrews class themselves with those who reject the Sabbath for the same reason.

The first-century apostle did not even have access to the time plan of the heavenly sanctuary. It was sealed away in Daniel's prophecies, not to be revealed "'until the end time'" (Dan. 12:9).

God never intended to repeat in Hebrews what had been long established by Daniel and Leviticus. We must accept God's Word on its own terms and be satisfied.

Atonement Meant More

But if Hebrews was not intended to teach that the Day of Atonement began at the cross, why are there so many references to Christ's atoning sacrifice? We must recall that atonement was not limited to the Day of Atonement. Atoning sacrifices were offered on other holy days too.[2] Atonement was a continuous function accomplished in three phases: (1) consecration of the sanctuary system, (2) the covering of sin, and (3) cleansing the sanctuary. In the establishment of the new sanctuary system, the apostle needed to show how Christ fitted into each of these several functions of atonement.

At the beginning of its services the sanctuary must be inaugurated. This involved the anointing of the priesthood in a consecration ceremony that included entering the Most Holy Place (Ex. 30:26-30). So the apostle points out that Christ was anointed by the Father (Heb. 1:9). Then he continues by contrasting the old-covenant inauguration with the new: "But when Christ appeared as a high priest of the good things to come, He entered through the greater and more perfect tabernacle, not made with hands, that is to say, not of this creation; and not through the blood of goats and calves, but through His own blood, He entered the holy place once for all, having obtained eternal redemption" (chap. 9:11, 12).

How do we know that Jesus made this entrance into the presence of God for inauguration and not to fulfill the Day of Atonement? Because a calf was sacrificed with a goat for atonement on inauguration (see Lev. 9:8, 15), not on Yom

Kippur.[3] Christ is here beginning His heavenly priesthood.

To Apply, Not Repeat

On the cross Jesus had been "displayed publicly as a propitiation [atonement] in His blood through faith" (Rom. 3:25). Calvary was the complete sacrifice, "the source of eternal salvation," "to all those who obey Him" (Heb. 5:9) in faith. Christ's sacrifice provided an infinite reservoir of atonement "that He might become a merciful and faithful high priest in things pertaining to God, to make propitiation for the sins of the people" (chap. 2:17).

The once-for-all-time sacrifice did not finish Christ's ministry of atonement. He inaugurated another "once for all" (chap. 9:12) ministry—not to repeat, but to apply, that eternal redemption. In our appreciation for the first "once for all," let us not forget His next phase of atonement in the heavenly holy places, where Jesus "always [continually] lives to make intercession" for us (chap. 7:25).

This continual ministry of Christ was foretold in the daily work of the priests: "For every high priest is appointed to offer both gifts and sacrifices; hence it is necessary that this high priest also have something to offer" (chap. 8:3). Everything in the old sanctuary system was " 'according to the pattern' " (verse 5) of what Christ would be doing, for those on earth did "serve a copy and shadow of the heavenly things" (verse 5). We have seen this pattern evident in both the inaugural anointing and the continual intercession of Christ's priesthood.

Cleansing Heaven's Temple

What about the final function of atonement—would Christ cleanse the heavenly sanctuary? How could it be otherwise? Cleansing the sanctuary on the day of judgment was the most important function of the high priesthood. How could Christ fulfill the symbol if He omitted this essential act?

Besides, "intercession inevitably points to judgment,"[4] for warnings abound throughout Hebrews that our response to Christ's atonement determines our judgment. Such as this one: "How much severer punishment do you think he will deserve who has trampled under foot the Son of God, and has regarded as unclean the blood of the covenant . . . ? 'The Lord will judge His people' " (chap. 10:29, 30).

Clearly there must be a final phase to consummate Christ's ministry of intercession. But is the future cleansing of the sanctuary explicitly stated in Hebrews? Yes: "Therefore it was necessary for the copies of the things in the heavens to be cleansed with these, but the heavenly things themselves with better sacrifices than these" (chap. 9:23).

First, notice that the heavenly things would be cleansed. This is not the purifying of sin by Christ's sacrifice on the cross, but the cleansing of the heavenly temple during Christ's priesthood. And the cleansing of the earthly is said to be a copy of the way the heavenly would be cleansed.[5] *This explicitly requires a parallel between the two sanctuaries in their cleansing.* We are to learn about how the heavenly sanctuary would be cleansed by the way the earthly sanctuary was cleansed.

Through the daily intercession, guilt from confessing believers accumulated in the sanctuary. Finally it was cleansed on the Day of Atonement. This prefigured what would happen in heaven, we are informed. Since His ascension and inauguration, our High Priest has been covering Christian confession with His continual intercession. Finally He will cleanse the heavenly sanctuary, as did the high priest in the example of the earthly.

"The context is clear—Christ has now appeared in the presence of God ministering in our behalf (verse 24) to put away sin, which is made possible by the benefits of His atoning sacrifice (verse 26). . . . It is here that the Day of Atonement imagery in Hebrews is most profound and justified, having its relevance in the complete removal of sin, after which Christ will appear a second time—not as a sin bearer, but without sin to them who expect Him for salvation (verse 28)." [6]

After this cleansing of heaven's sanctuary is completed, just as the high priest emerged before a waiting Israel after purifying the sanctuary, "so Christ . . . shall appear a second time for salvation without reference to sin, to those who eagerly await Him" (verse 28).

Eighteen-Century Separation?

"But wait!" someone interjects. "We learned from Hebrews 9:12 that Christ at His ascension entered 'once for all' into the presence of the Father to fulfill the Old Testament inaugural service in the Most Holy Place. Haven't we taught that Christ was separated from the Father's throne by a veil for eighteen centuries?"

According to Hebrews 10:20, the veil of the old sanctuary symbolized the flesh of Christ. When His heart broke on the cross this veil was torn, thus opening a new and living way to the throne of grace. Before this, only the high priest could enter the Holiest, and that only once a year. But now all of us have continual access to the Father's throne.

This is what we celebrate with the broken communion bread. Catholics interpret this new-covenant symbol too literally, forgetting that it means nothing in itself and only represents something greater. Let us not make a similar mistake with the old-covenant symbol of the same body of Christ. Both the veil and the bread have no reality in themselves—they both are teaching tools to represent the access to God's presence we have through the broken body of Jesus.

Real Pages Turning?

And what about books of judgment? Some people are extremely literalistic, thinking it irreverent that God may have a celestial videotape of some kind instead of an actual book with pages to turn. These folks do not realize that the symbol itself is a scroll—not a book with pages. What is the reality it conveys? Simply that we are accountable to God in everything; "there is significance even in the 'idle word' (Matt. 12:36 [K.J.V.]), for our spontaneous, unplanned, and unself-conscious talk is often a distressingly accurate reflection of our inner attitudes and our real identity."[7]

Others, of course, go to the other extreme and deny the heavenly realities these symbols represent. Although the ceremonial system was "only a shadow of the good things to come and not the very form of things" (Heb. 10:1), every symbol is important and represents some aspect of Christ's work for us. "Greater and more perfect" (chap. 9:11) indeed is the heavenly tabernacle—different, but real! The sanctuary in heaven is as real as the New Jerusalem. But also it is just as proportionately more glorious than the Temple on earth as the Holy City is more magnificent than Palestine's capital symbol.

So the earthly Temple with its veil was a symbol of the heavenly system but not a Xerox copy. And it was given to help us understand the priesthood of Jesus on our behalf—not to show us what heaven looks like.

The General Conference Sanctuary Review Committee, in its consensus document, reported that among church leaders at Glacier View "there is basic agreement that Christ at His ascension entered into the very presence of God. . . . But we do deny that His entrance into the presence of God (1) precludes a first-apartment phase of ministry or (2) marks the beginning of the second [1844] phase of His ministry."[8]

Sprinkling Dried Blood?

At this point we must consider two objections proposed by Desmond Ford to deny the 1844 change in Christ's priesthood.

First, Ford insists that because the atoning blood shed at Calvary would have dried up before 1844, it cannot be used in our time to sprinkle the heavenly sanctuary during the second phase of Christ's priesthood:

"The blood sprinkled on the mercy seat was warm. It had to be uncoagulated [unclotted], or sprinkling would have been impossible. . . . While Adventists have realized that the slaying of the goat on the Day of Atonement was not fulfilled in 1844, they have endeavored to separate the aspersion [sprinkling of the blood] on the mercy seat till that time—something exegetically, theologically, and logically unsound."[9]

If this is true, the blood would have had to be rushed into heaven *immediately*—minutes after Christ died. Any delay, even for a few days, would have made the sprinkling of warm blood impossible.

"This argument is characterized by an extreme literalism and rigid typology. Although Dr. Ford refuses to recognize the validity of typology [symbolism] in establishing Christ's two-phased ministry in the heavenly sanctuary, he himself does not hesitate to employ the same approach to substantiate his own viewpoints."[10]

If Christ could plead His shed blood for sinners all these years, why could He not cleanse the sanctuary, too? The judgment scene of Revelation 4 and 5 shows "a Lamb standing, as if slain," before the throne (chap. 5:6). Evidently the blood never loses its power.

Better Blood

Now let us examine another major objection from Ford to the 1844 change in Christ's priesthood. "The Day of Atonement is applied throughout Hebrews to what Christ had already done by the Cross and His ascension to heaven. Hebrews does not teach that the Day of Atonement points to some event eighteen centuries then future. It teaches the opposite." [11]

We have already seen evidence of a two-phase priesthood of Christ in Hebrews. But how do we explain its references to the Day of Atonement? William Johnsson, editor of the *Adventist Review*, proposes a logical answer:

"The apostle here definitely does *not* deal with the work of Christ in the heavenly tabernacle from a time perspective. What he is concerned with is one supreme idea—*the all-sufficiency of His death*. He contrasts the Old Testament sacrifices with the one Superlative Sacrifice. To do this he takes the high point of the Old Testament religious year—Yom Kippur—and argues that even on this day the sacrifices did not resolve the sin problem, as shown by the annual reenactment of Yom Kippur. That is, the highest point of the Old Testament cultic year could not purge sin away. Obviously, if the Day of Atonement services were inadequate, how much more all other sacrifices. . . . The argument of Hebrews, then, does not deny the SDA sanctuary doctrine, because basically it does not address the issue. We may say, particularly on the strength of 9:23, that it allows for it. But we cannot dilute the apostle's emphasis on *one point* in time—the once-for-all sacrifice of Calvary—by importing into the context considerations of subsequent events in history." [12]

So "the leitmotif [dominant theme] of the sacrificial argument of Hebrews (8:1-10:18) is the *better blood* rather than the Day of Atonement. [13] The veiled threat is vanquished.

Further Proof

Further confirmation from both Testaments that final events, not the cross, fulfill the Day of Atonement is its placement within the cycle of sanctuary services. Seven annual holy days, symbolizing proceedings in salvation history, were divided into two clusters—the first four were celebrated in springtime, during the early part of the Jewish calendar; the final three were reserved until the time of reaping the harvest. According to the New Testament, the spring feasts symbolized events in connection with Christ's first advent: (1) Passover—the crucifixion of Jesus (1 Cor. 5:7); (2) Feast of Unleavened Bread—our repentance and faith in appreciation of the cross (verses 7, 8); (3) Ceremony of the First Fruits—Christ's resurrection and ascension to God on our behalf (1 Cor. 5:7, 8); (4) Pentecost—the outpouring of the Holy Spirit upon God's church in response to our commitment to Jesus and our fellowship with one another (Acts 2:1-4).

After the first crowded schedule of feasts, a long stretch of months followed without celebration of any annual event. Then in the time of harvest, during the seventh month came the final three convocations of the religious year. Notice their special application to the second advent of Jesus: (5) Feast of Trumpets—the proclamation of approaching judgment (Revelation 8 and 9); (6) Day of Atonement—judgment from the inner temple (chap. 11:19); (7) Feast of Tabernacles—the harvest at Christ's coming (chap. 14:14, 15).

The timing of this forecast of salvation history is both striking and significant. M. L. Andreasen observes: "The type is perfect even as to time. The lamb died on the evening of the fourteenth day of Abib. On the sixteenth, the 'morrow after the sabbath' [Lev. 23;11, K.J.V.], the first fruits, which had previously been cut down, were presented before the Lord. Christ died Friday evening. He rested in the grave over the Sabbath. The 'morrow after the sabbath' 'Christ the firstfruits' [1 Cor. 15:23, K.J.V.] was raised from the grave, and presented Himself before the Lord for acceptance." [14]

The chronological accuracy marking the fulfillment of the first feasts is continued with Pentecost: "As the wave loaves were offered fifty days after the wave sheaf was presented, so there were just fifty days between the resurrection of Christ and the outpouring of the Spirit on Pentecost." [15]

Since God has displayed such care for chronology, is it not reasonable to connect the long gap that separates the first group of feasts from the final group of feasts with the long gap that separates the first century from our last days? Does this not indicate that God foreknew a long delay in the Second Advent?

True, a "doctrine cannot be established by types or prophetic interpretation—these may only be used to illustrate and confirm what is clearly taught elsewhere, and in nonsymbolic language." [16] But we are not speculating with symbols here. The New Testament explicitly plants the fulfillment of the first feasts in the days of the apostles. The final feasts, with their Second Advent significance, are *not* tied by the New Testament to the first century—they are left unfulfilled for the time of the end.

So Hebrews is in harmony with its companions of inspiration. Once again we have been confronted with compelling confirmation of Adventist doctrine. Praise God!

After all this discussion about priests and feasts, let us cherish a quiet moment with Jesus, our friendly High Priest. The heartbeat of Hebrews is Christ's tender love for His sinful, struggling people. He who Himself suffered, sympathizes now with our weaknesses. At infinite cost He has provided us limitless access to the throne of grace, for mercy. Thank God for mercy—we need it more than oxygen. And grace to help—we need that, too, being utterly weak sheep. So may "the God of peace, who brought up from the dead the great Shepherd of the sheep through the blood of the eternal covenant, even Jesus our Lord, equip you in every good thing to do His will, working in us that which is pleasing in His sight, through Jesus Christ, to whom be the glory forever and ever. Amen" (Heb. 13:20, 21).

14 Sabbath Wrest

America is being born again! Religion is emerging as the dominant force in U.S. culture and possibly U.S. politics, according to a major survey of American values in the 1980s. "We had no idea we'd find this. But there it was," exclaimed project director John C. Pollock. "Our findings suggest that the increasing impact of religion . . . could change the face of America." [1]

It has happened here before. In fact, this would be the fourth time a national revival has swept through American society. In the 1740s came the famous Great Awakening, with its emphasis on personal and national morality. Another religious earthquake shook the early nineteenth century, helping to lay the moral groundwork for the antislavery activism of the next generation. The third came near the birth of the twentieth century in the revolt of the Southern "Bible Belt" against the secular influences of the Northeast industrial revolution. Revival has swept through America every seventy-five to one hundred years. The time has come to expect another great awakening.

Our national spirit is ripe. Having tuned out the freaked-out sixties, we are likewise disillusioned with the useless humanism of the secular seventies. Like the prodigal returning from his affair with a far-off land, we are once again becoming one nation under God, this time with one crucial variance of immense prophetic significance: Our present awakening "already differs from all three predecessors in one extremely important characteristic—ecumenicalism. Fundamentalist Protestants are by no means the only group aroused by moral issues like abortion, school prayer, pornography, homosexuality, sexual permissiveness, atheism in the classroom, and so forth. With conservative Catholics and Jews also up in arms, *denominationalism seems less important now than shared moral and religious tradition.*" [2]

So conservative Protestants, Catholics, and even Jews are now working together to reunite God and country. Can this be anything but the ecumenical movement Adventists have long expected?

A new day indeed is here. Ever since Lord Baltimore split the Protestant coastline with his new Catholic colony, America had been embroiled in an uncivil religious war. Historically we have hissed and barked in the name of Christ after the manner of alley cats and stray dogs engaging in fervent battle. The current easement of hostilities is nothing less than incredible. What brought this dramatic shift in attitude?

The Charismatic Connection

Twenty years ago Catholics opened the door with Vatican II. At the beginning of that historic church council, Pope John XXIII prayed for a Pentecostal revival to renew the church.[3] Meanwhile, Protestants themselves were being turned on to a new Pentecostal movement erupting unexpectedly in many churches. Late in the sixties this charismatic revival spread to the Catholic Church, and in 1975 it was unofficially but unmistakably blessed by Pope Paul VI.[4] Many Catholics now believe this ecumenical infusion of spiritual power is God's answer to the pope's prayer at Vatican II.[5]

For the first time Protestants worshiped together with Roman Catholics at huge charismatic rallies where everyone sang, "We are one in the Spirit." The pervading feeling is "We're not so different after all when we can praise the Lord together for the new life we share in the Spirit."

Why is the charismatic movement so warmly welcomed by Rome? Although its origins are Protestant, "Catholics who have accepted Pentecostal spirituality have found it to be fully in harmony with their traditional faith and life. They experience it, not as a borrowing from an alien religion, but as a connatural development of their own."[6]

Moses and the Beast

Not surprisingly, in their new alignment with Catholicism Protestants have developed respect for strict morality and law. Radio preachers, upset over pervading immorality, are working hard to undo the damage they caused by years of teaching that faith in Christ abolishes the law. Following the pendulum of human nature, many are shifting from Calvinism to the other extreme, Catholicism. Evangelicals are mobilizing to enforce the Ten Commandments upon American society. New groups have mushroomed, such as the Christian Action Council, "committed to standing for God's righteousness in calling our nation to bring our human laws into harmony with His Divine Law."[7]

Many earnest and sincere Christians have been deceived by this morality movement. The world has been allured by Pope John Paul II. Before Communists, who deny God and His commandments, he stands up for Christ and His moral law. No wonder Billy Graham considers him to be the "moral leader of the world." Jerry Falwell calls the Pope "the best hope we Baptists ever had."[8] And why not? Thirty percent of his Moral Majority income comes from Catholics.[9]

"We are seeing a political alliance between Roman Catholics and conservative Protestants that could have a profound impact,"[10] observes Falwell. In the light of such statements it is incredible that many Adventists join Catholics in funding Falwell. But Adventists like what he says about God's law. If he would only keep the seventh day, many imagine, he would have a perfect program. Why does Falwell's organization reject Sabbath rest? Despite many worthwhile concerns about morality, his movement is nothing but corporate legalism. National salvation by law—the new song of Moses and the beast.

This abuse of God's law by Sundaykeepers is somewhat ironic. Sabbathkeeping often has been judged legalism by those who reject Adventism. Are we all now guilty of righteousness by law? Let us trace the meaningful roots of the Sabbath and its first-day counterpart. Then we will understand how Sabbath conflict will unleash the closing crisis.

The Roots of Rest

Why was the Sabbath "'made for man'" (Mark 2:27)? As a yoke of the old covenant? How could the Sabbath be an expression of works when the word itself is derived from the Hebrew *shabbath,* meaning to "cease, desist, rest" [11]—quite the opposite of work? This Sabbath rest roots in the beginning, when God rested in His finished Creation: "Thus the heavens and the earth were completed, and all their hosts. And by the seventh day God completed His work which He had done; and He rested on the seventh day from all His work which He had done. Then God blessed the seventh day and sanctified it, because in it He rested from all His work which God had created and made" (Gen. 2:1-3).

Man, being the crowning act of Creation, was not in existence when the work was being accomplished. He contributed nothing and had no right to rest. But even though undeserving, he was invited anyway to join God's celebration of His finished work.

So Sabbathkeeping means resting in God's accomplishments as if they were our own—not competing with them. This is also the good news of Calvary. Besides Creation, the other great act of God for the human race is redemption. As sundown approached on that other Friday, Christ on the cross cried, "'It is finished!'" This was not a wail of despair, but the triumphant proclamation of a completed work. Mission accomplished! Mankind redeemed!

Christ once more rested on the Sabbath, this time in the tomb, in honor of His finished work. At the resurrection His Father welcomed Him back into heaven and received at the same time the whole human race. But God's acceptance of us in the Beloved is not enough for our salvation. "By grace you have been saved through faith" (Eph. 2:8). We must accept our acceptance or be lost. The Sabbath serves Christians with a weekly invitation—and a warning—to rest in the accomplishments of Christ's life, not in our own. Simply stated, Sabbathkeeping means we believe in Jesus. In a world of atheists and doubters, we believe He is our Creator. And surrounded by self-dependence and legalism, we trust instead in His salvation.

Sabbath rest in Christ is beautifully presented in the New Testament book of Hebrews. After chapter 3 recounts the fatal unbelief of those who failed to enter Canaan, a warning comes for Jewish Christians to avoid likewise falling short of gospel rest. In this context of resting in God's salvation, the seventh-day Sabbath is introduced, when God's "works were finished from the foundation of the world" and He "rested on the seventh day from all His works" (chap. 4:3, 4). Then comes the sad history of Jewish failure to enter this Sabbath rest that God had earned for them. Even after Joshua finally led them into Canaan they were not yet into Sabbath rest. Being external sabbatarians, the Jews did avoid business on the holy day, but they were not true Sabbathkeepers—they never entered the spirit of Sabbath rest.

This passage, when closely examined, clearly carries the seventh-day Sabbath into the Christian church. Verse 8 mentions "another day" David introduced. Another day besides what? The Sabbath, of course; the passage is still discussing the seventh-day rest. Did David's day replace the Sabbath day? On the contrary. He made true Sabbathkeeping possible by calling a time apart to repent and believe in God's salvation. Did the Jews ever become true Sabbathkeepers? Unfortunately not: "There remains therefore a Sabbath rest for the people of God" (verse 9). And what Sabbath rest is this that remains for New Testament Christians? "For the one who has entered His rest has himself also rested from his works, as God did from His" (verse 10). When did God rest from His works? On the seventh-day Sabbath. So this seventh-day Sabbath, says the apostle, remains for us so we can celebrate gospel rest.

There is no hint in Hebrews 4 that God replaced His sacred seventh-day with another symbol of rest. On the contrary, this chaper establishes the seventh-day Sabbath in the New Testament. Since verse 10 tells us to cease from our works "as God did from His," it explicitly points back to the Creation *sabbatismos* as the model for the Christian church.

But could the apostle be telling the Hebrews that their nation never kept the Sabbath? Yes. The Jews, who strictly observed the day, ignored its meaning. Hebrews 4 proves their need to begin true Sabbathkeeping by reminding them of a fact in their history. In David's day, four centuries after Joshua brought them across the Jordan, they still had not entered the rest represented by the Sabbath. They were external sabbatarians, not true Sabbathkeepers. Finally they crucified the Lord of the Sabbath and hurried home before sundown.

Remember the purpose of the book itself—helping Jewish Christians see Jesus in their heritage. The Hebrews had no problem with external religious observance; they needed to accept Christ in these ceremonies. Jesus as High Priest in the sanctuary system. And Jesus as Lord of the Sabbath.

Do Adventists likewise need to enter God's rest? When the meaning of Hebrews 4 is learned there will be power to proclaim the Sabbath more fully. Many fellow Christians will for the first time see light in Sabbathkeeping. What Joshua, David, and 1888 failed to get across is yet to be proclaimed through the three angels' messages of Revelation 14.

Why Then the Law?

If the Sabbath means entering God's rest, why is it included in the law? Is it not therefore legalism, after all? No, the Sabbath commandment is unique among the ten. It is the only one not an obvious moral duty. Why? Amid the law's stringent demands God offers us rest in the fourth commandment. The other nine tell us *what we must do for God* and neighbor. But the Sabbath instructs us to rest in *what God has done for us*. Exodus 20 reminds us of God's finished Creation on our behalf. Deuteronomy 5 invites us to rest on the Sabbath in memory of the redemption He accomplished for us.

Without the Sabbath, obedience would be legalism. But through rest in Christ's completed salvation we are filled with appreciation. Thus we reflect love to Him and to His children—which is the keeping of the law. The Sabbath frees us to honor the other commandments.

Now we see why " 'the Sabbath was made for man' " by the Son of man, who " 'is Lord even of the Sabbath' " (Mark 2:27, 28). The Sabbath is not a twenty-four-hour guard chain stretched across the end of the week to deny us of weekend fun! Instead, it is a joyous celebration of assurance that our Father has accepted us in Christ. Rather than being a work to earn salvation, the Sabbath memorializes the two greatest accomplishments of God for His children.

The Sabbath is the billboard of Calvary's freedom, the greatest teaching tool of the gospel. Every Friday afternoon your work goes down with the sun. This apparently violates the work ethic, which says to rest only when the work is finished. Why does the Sabbath require that we cease our works even while they are uncompleted? Because God finished His work and invites us, undeserving as we are, to share His rest. This is the gospel. We all come short. With Isaiah we cry, "Unclean! Undone!" But "in Him you have been made complete" (Col. 2:10). We rest in His accomplishments as if they were our own. This is Christianity.

Must we keep the Sabbath before we are accepted? No. Does this make the Sabbath optional? Well, is baptism a matter of preference? Almost every denomination has some form of baptism as a requirement for the Christian life. Is this legalism? No, baptism expresses one's choice to accept the achievements of Christ. So does the Sabbath. For one to know the meaning of baptism into Jesus and yet refuse it would be to reject salvation. " 'He who has believed and has been baptized shall be saved' " (Mark 16:16). Like one-time baptism, the Sabbath is a weekly symbol of living in Christ's rest. To refuse it is to refuse Him. You see how the Sabbath is a test of salvation, only, of course, for those who have had opportunity to understand this glorious truth as it is in Jesus.

The Antisabbath

What beautiful truth God gave us in Sabbath rest! You can imagine how Satan hates this weekly reminder of refuge in Christ. How could he destroy the Sabbath by making it appear spiritually illegitimate? Working through his mystery of iniquity, he invented the Sunday counterfeit to ruin our rest in Christ's atonement.

"Why was Sunday chosen? Because on that day Christ rose from the dead and the Holy Spirit descended upon the Apostles. The Resurrection was the greatest miracle which Christ wrought, and demonstrated in a most striking manner the divinity of Christ and of His Church. On Pentecost the Holy Spirit entered the Church to be the source of its divine life and to abide with it forever." [12]

So instead of Sabbath rest in the atoning blood of Christ, the devil substituted worship of the new-life miracle made possible by Christ's resurrection and the powerful impartation of God's grace through His Spirit at Pentecost. The devil ingeniously robbed the cross of its glory by worshiping the grace that sanctifies the believer: "The Sunday assembly and Eucharist of the Church are a celebration of the re-creation of men." [13] This obsession with man's acquired holiness leads directly into papal perfectionism.

You see the difference between God's rest and its counterfeit. The Sabbath finds refuge in Christ's accomplishments. True obedience stems from forgiveness through His blood. Sundaykeeping is based not on the cross, but on the life of new creation that powerfully changes our lives to supposedly qualify us for heaven. So Sunday observance represents "legalism by faith," fundamental to both the Pentecostal movement and Catholicism.

Hijack on the Gospel Freeway

To understand Sunday worship we must go back to the Garden of Eden. No sooner did the devil trap our parents at the tree than he sprang his second deception—inducing them to rely upon their own experience to cover their guilt. Not wishing to run around in guilty shame, they took what the Lord had grown with their cooperation (Adam tended the garden, you recall) and tried to cover themselves (Gen. 3:7). Salvation by works. It did not work. God had a better idea.

After sharing the gospel with them (verse 15), "the Lord God made garments of skin for Adam and his wife, and clothed them" (verse 21). What was happening? God had decreed that on the day of their sin they would surely die. Now this death was executed in the sacrifice of an innocent substitute, symbolizing Christ. From that day forward the guilty pair lived by faith in their substitute by wearing its skin to cover their shame. No more fig leaves. The covering God provided had not one stitch of human contribution.

So God has no use for human attempts to cover sinfulness by sewing together fig leaves of sanctification He has grown with our faith. Rest is not something we manufacture for God. It is not even something God produces within our lives. Christ's innocent blood was shed on our behalf to provide a completed refuge that we enter. Our part is to admit our lost condition, forsake both the nudity of presumption and the fig leaves of legalism, and accept the robe of redemption provided ready-made without a stitch of human devising. So our hope is in the perfect sacrifice of Christ, not in the transforming power of His grace.

Grace will grow in our lives. But that change never becomes the basis of our relationship. For example, children grow in the gifts their parents provide. Life depends upon whether they receive nourishing grace, but their acceptance in the family has nothing to do with fulfilling any growth quota. I doubt whether any parent on earth has such a program, and neither does our Father in heaven.

Once saved, always saved? Not at all. We must walk with Jesus in a trustful and obedient relationship, continually resting in His laurels—not our own. This is the message of the Sabbath that Satan attempts to supplant with his Sunday.

After God revealed His mercy to our unworthy parents in Eden, the devil was not deterred in his war against the gospel. Fiendishly determined to abolish the life-or-death principle of trusting the blood of a substitute, he again incited the offering of human fruit—grown by the power of God, of course. But God could not accept Cain's legalism by faith. He never has respect for our sanctification as fit righteousness, even though He provides the power that grows both fruit and fig leaves. Only to the blood of His Lamb can the Lord show respect. If we refuse to rest in Christ's accomplishments as our own, God must sadly reject us. It is no accident that many Eastern religions offer fruit in their heathen worship. We must never do the same.

Come Unto Rome and Wrest

So the gospel and its counterfeit have been with us since the first day of sin. Both are symbolized every week in worship. Sabbathkeeping means being clothed by the Lamb for trusting in His blood. Sunday worship is the end-time equivalent of fig leaves and sacrificial fruit.

Final conflict between opposing sabbaths is evident in the New Testament. Remember the judgment scene of Revelation 4 and 5? The Sabbath is vitally involved in this court of the great cosmic controversy. God is declared worthy of honor because He created all things (chap. 4:11). Christ is proclaimed worthy because by His blood He purchased redemption (chap. 5:9). The Sabbath is the special memorial of both divine accomplishments. Therefore it represents evidence that vindicates God over the challenge of the enemy.

The Sabbath is also important in vindicating the saints. The central question in the judgment is " 'Who is worthy?' " (verse 2). Only the Lamb—the Lord of the Sabbath—is judged worthy. We must enter His rest to pass the judgment. So true Sabbathkeeping will be essential evidence that we live in Christ.

Sabbath rest is inherent within each of the three angels' messages of Revelation 14. The first calls us to worship the Creator, " 'who made the heaven and the earth and sea' " (verse 7)—explicitly quoting the fourth commandment. The second message announces the fall of Babylon, which has fermented the gospel of Sabbath rest into the wine of Sunday works. The third warns us away from the beast, who robs his followers of rest day and night (verses 9-11). Their false worship expels Sabbath rest. Those who overcome the beast "keep the commandments of God and their faith in Jesus" (verse 12). Through our Sabbath rest in Christ we honor the law.

The Test of Rest

So the Sabbath wll be the test of rest. Adventists often misunderstand how the law will be abused by Sundaykeepers. Since faith in Christ establishes the law (Rom. 3:31), legalism must abolish it. Persecution will come in the name of God's law—Paul warned that the persecuting son of the flesh comes from Mount Sinai (Gal. 4:25-30). In a backlash of righteousness against the lawless decay of society, those who rest in Christ will be misunderstood and face extermination by legalistic Babylon.

So the test at the last is rest, just as it was at the beginning. We who observe the Sabbath must remember that the seventh day in itself means nothing. Unfortunately, the devil has infected even Sabbathkeepers with Sunday-style legalism. Remember the self-righteous Pharisee? He prayed, " ' "God, I thank Thee that I am not like other people" ' " (Luke 18:11). Evidently the legalists who crucified Christ did not look within for their strength—they trusted God for enabling grace to compete with the law. " 'Give glory to God,' " they ordered the restored blind man (John 9:24). Why did these strict Sabbatarians crucify the Lord of the Sabbath? They would not come to Him and rest in His accomplishments. But the poor publican who cried, " ' "God, be merciful to me, the sinner!" ' " (Luke 18:13) had the true spirit that should characterize the Sabbathkeeper. He had entered rest.

Our choice is simple: salvation in Christ's Sabbath rest, or doom in Sabbatarian or Sunday legalism. As the world is hijacked by Satan in the name of God's law, the Lord of Sabbath rest invites us: "I have achieved your morality; come unto Me and rest. Lose the law for My sake, and you will find each wonderful commandment fulfilling in your life."

15 A Nonprophet Organization?

T
he year 1888 brought high drama to the Seventh-day Adventist Church. An unprecedented crisis confronting the General Conference session seemed to jeopardize its very existence. Unity had been shattered, and a split appeared imminent. According to some historians, without God's ministry in Ellen White the denomination might not have survived that Minneapolis meeting long enough to welcome the twentieth century.

It was a classic struggle over theology. After decades of debating doctrine, Adventists had developed an affection for argument. Proud of their skill in wielding His Sword, they forgot their dependence upon mercy. Soon they were the lawyers of God, no longer His lovers. Many became confirmed legalists. Striking proof of this is an engraving entitled "The Way of Life," brought out by James White in 1876. Towering above everything else was the law, dwarfing even the cross. This portrayed the mind-set of many in the church.

But all were not captured by the spirit of the day. During the 1880s a rediscovery of faith in Jesus emerged like spring out of winter, bursting through the legalism that had snowed some under. Ellet J. Waggoner and Alonzo T. Jones, each an Adventist editor and minister, intensively investigated the law in its relation to the righteousness of Christ. Although they conducted their studies independently, they arrived at similar conclusions.

As they shared their newfound faith, "certain Battle Creek leaders had the feeling that these 'two young men' . . . were out to 'revolutionize' the teachings of the denomination on certain points—along rather 'heretical' lines." [1] Battle lines were drawn by 1886, when General Conference president George Butler published a pamphlet opposing their views. Confrontation was imminent.

A Nonprophet Organization?

Meanwhile Ellen White was also growing in her understanding of salvation. In 1883 she boldly commissioned a new engraving to replace the one produced by her late husband. The difference between the two was dramatic. She had revised both the picture and its caption, entitling it "CHRIST the Way of Life." The cross reigned supreme over everything, even the law. None could miss the point. Not everyone liked her new emphasis.

Ever increasing in her understanding of the gospel, Ellen White during the 1880s worked hard to purge the church of the legalistic leaven of the Pharisees. She lamented, "As a people, we have preached the law until we are as dry as the hills of Gilboa that had neither dew nor rain."[2] Some of the brethren were not happy with her new light. By 1888 the countdown reached blast-off.

Waggoner knew there would be trouble. But he did not realize how soon it would hit him. Upon his arrival in Minneapolis, a blackboard was already in place advertising the opposing positions. Iowa Conference president J. H. Morrison had fixed his signature on one side, leaving a challenge for Waggoner to sign the other. Waggoner refused. He had not come to engage in debate. He just wanted to share Jesus.

As Waggoner and Jones launched their presentations the cry went forth to "stand by the old landmarks!" A motion was made to quench discussion of the troublesome subject, but Ellen White blocked this move with a warning from heaven: "I never was more alarmed than at the present time."[3] When entreated to silence the heretics, she instead endorsed them: "If the ministers will not receive the light, I want to give the people a chance; perhaps they may receive it. God did not raise me up [from illness] to come across the plains to speak to you and you sit here to question His message and question whether Sister White is the same as she used to be in years gone by."[4]

Evidently the rumor was spreading that the church was becoming a nonprophet organization. How ironic! Even while being confronted with her compelling example of ministry, many were inclined to dismiss her as an unfit prophet. Why? She showed a disturbing eagerness to learn and grow, even if it meant upgrading her appreciation of the landmarks. They could not accept that prophets could change their minds and mature in their teaching. She replied: "The Lord has been pleased to give me great light, *yet I know that He leads other minds, and opens to them the mysteries of His Word,* and I want to receive every ray of light that God shall send me, though it should come through the humblest of His servants."[5]

John Grew Too

Remember John the Baptist? " 'A prophet? Yes, . . .' " Jesus informs us, " 'more than a prophet. . . . There has not arisen anyone greater than John the Baptist' " (Matt. 11:9-11). Yet John grew in interpreting his own message. At first he expected a different kind of Messiah from what Christ turned out to be, one to " 'thoroughly clear His threshing floor; and . . . gather His wheat into the barn, but . . . burn up the chaff with unquenchable fire' " (chap. 3:12). However, instead of cleansing society of its evildoers, Christ allowed tares to ripen with wheat until a future harvest at His coming.

Christ's performing the opposite of his expectations finally led the prophet even to doubt that Jesus was indeed the Saviour: " 'Are You the Expected One, or shall we look for someone else?' " (chap. 11:3). In addition to misunderstanding the nature of the Messiah's mission, the prophet suffered strains of legalism. "John the Baptist did not understand the nature of Christ's kingdom,"[6] Ellen White notes. Naturally his teaching was deficient, so "the disciples of John had not a clear understanding of Christ's work. . . . They . . . even hoped to be justified by the works of the law."[7] When his audience asked what to do about their sins, the prophet gave them work to do—share their tunics, be content with their wages, and quit robbing taxpayers (see Luke 3:11-14). John preached repentance but said nothing about salvation by grace. Paul had to rebaptize some of his converts because of the prophet's immature theology (Acts 19:1-5).

Did the prophet's imperfect doctrine disqualify him from being a true messenger? Jesus did not think so. John admirably fulfilled his purpose by preparing the people, identifying Jesus as the Messiah, and baptizing Him. Then why did God permit John to preach immature theology along with truth?

The prophet had to teach on the kindergarten level. God's people were not ready for the full message, so He gave them a prophet who could *meet them on their own level and lead them* to the point where they finally could appreciate the gospel. God never intended for John to preach with the same insight that Paul would later on. The people were not ready for the lofty gospel of the apostle. There were many things even Jesus wanted to say but could not because the people were not able to comprehend and accept (see John 16:12). God called a prophet who shared many misconceptions with the people so that they could relate to his teaching.

Refreshing Frankness

Likewise with Ellen White. She did not always enjoy a mature understanding of truth. In fact, according to Robert Olson, of the White Estate, she "did not at first understand the meaning of the 'open door' in her February, 1845, vision."[8] She had previously mistaken her December, 1844, vision: "That 17-year-old Ellen should misinterpret one of her visions should elicit no surprise when one remembers that the Bible prophets found it necessary to study their own writings. . . . At one time the apostle Peter mistakenly believed in a shut door."[9]

Olson continues: "The 1846 and 1847 printings of Ellen White's first vision included the sentence in the box above ["It was just as impossible for them to get on the path again and go to the City, as all the wicked world which God had rejected"]. The 1851 printing of the same vision omitted the sentence. Why was it omitted? Ellen White no doubt realized that the passage had been misunderstood by some of her readers, as well as by herself."[10]

Olson's frankness is refreshing. It has been an agonizing struggle for Adventists to acknowledge the reality of Ellen White's need to grow. But why? If we see growth in the greatest of prophets, can we not accept it in a modern-day one? Just think, what if God had given the message of 1888 in 1844? People would have choked! It was hard enough to swallow forty-four years later. In the ministry of His servant Ellen White, God met His people down in the dumps after the great Disappointment, brought hope, and led them into the green pastures of a wonderful message. Since Ellen White was indeed a true prophet, we should expect to see a pattern of growth in her writings to correspond with the growing capacity for maturity in the Advent Movement.

Another clear example of doctrinal growth is Ellen White's understanding of the Holy Spirit. "Before 1896, the Spirit of God is never spoken of as a 'Person' in the writings of Sister White; after that date, 'He' is several times so referred to." [11] Now think it through. Either the Holy Spirit changed from an influence to a person in the year 1896, or Ellen White reversed an incorrect doctrinal position. You know the answer.

That this prophet also needed growth in her understanding of God's character is obvious from her *Appeal to Youth,* published in 1864: "God loves honest-hearted, truthful children, but cannot love those who are dishonest." "The Lord loves those little children who try to do right, and He has promise that they shall be in His kingdom. But wicked children God does not love. . . . When you feel tempted to speak impatient and fretful, remember the Lord sees you, and will not love you if you do wrong." [12]

Now compare the above with the following, published twenty-eight years later (after 1888): "Do not teach your children that God does not love them when they do wrong; teach them that He loves them so that it grieves His tender Spirit to see them in transgression." [13]

Here we have two different concepts of God's love. Does it matter which way we teach our children to feel about God? What encouraged the prodigal son to come home?

Have you noticed that Ellen White is always moving in the right direction? What else would we expect from a true prophet?

She also grew in her understanding of prophecy. Back in the 1888 edition of *The Great Controversy* she wrote that Babylon "cannot refer to the Romish Church, for that church has been in a fallen condition for many centuries." [14] But in her 1911 revision she inserted a significant word: Babylon "cannot refer to the Roman Church alone, for that church has been in a fallen condition for many centuries." [15]

"The pastor did not rob the bank." "The pastor did not rob the bank *alone.*" Do you see the difference?

Pious Criminals

Many Adventists invoke the doctrinal authority of Ellen White in order to escape the bother of Bible study: "Sister White taught the investigative judgment, and that settles it for me!"

Sounds good. But can this be a pious excuse to escape wrestling with difficult Bible passages? Was the gift of prophecy given to make us lazy? "Many have become lazy and criminally neglectful in regard to the searching of the Scriptures, and they are as destitute of the Spirit of God as of the knowledge of His word." [16]

As a pastor I have observed that some of Ellen White's most vocal defenders

THE WAY OF LIFE, From Paradise Lost to Paradise Restored

CHRIST The Way of Life

are almost ignorant of what she really taught. When they are questioned, it becomes apparent that not only do they neglect their Bibles—they have not studied her books in years. Like the Pharisees with Moses, they defend their prophet in name only and, with the Samaritan woman at the well, worship what they do not know (see John 4:22). They are much more familiar with *TV Guide* or the sports section of the daily paper. Hypocrites love to hide behind a mirage of denominational patriotism. But God is not deceived or mocked.

Television faith healers want audiences to "pray for us and please support this ministry." They always mention prayer before the money, but everyone knows which is really important to them. It just sounds better to put prayer first. Even so, many sincere Adventists speak of "studying the Bible and the Spirit of Prophecy." The Bible is always mentioned first, but the bottom line is usually Ellen White. Most times they are not conscious of making Ellen White their final authority over Scripture. But when an apparent conflict appears between the Bible and the prophet, they seem to prefer the word of the prophet—even while claiming the Bible only as their rule of faith. How do they manage this? Through circular reasoning:

"Why do I believe in Ellen White? Because everything she says agrees with the Bible. So everything in the Bible can be tested by her writings. I rely upon her interpretation of Scripture. This means that in principle I accept 'the Bible and the Bible only,' since everything she says agrees with the Bible."

Catholics use similar reasoning: "Why do I believe whatever the pope says? Because everything he says agrees with the Bible. So everything in the Bible [including Sunday worship] can be tested by the teachings of the pope. I rely upon his interpretation of Scripture. This means that in principle I accept 'the Bible and the Bible only,' since everything the pope says agrees with the Bible."

You see the problem. Anything that defines Scripture replaces it as the final authority. The fundamental issue of the Protestant Reformation was that the Bible must be its own interpreter. It was not that the pope was a bad interpreter of Scripture and now we must find a better umpire. The Bible itself is its own final word. It contains the entire system of truth. Ellen White repeatedly declared, "The Bible is to be presented as the word of the infinite God, as the end of all controversy and the foundation of all faith." [17]

This was demonstrated in the 1888 controversy over the law in Galatians. Although Ellen White had previously supported the traditional view, [18] now as always she was willing to walk in the light. This disturbed some of the brethren who remembered a misplaced manuscript she had written on the matter under discussion. Here is her reply: "Has he [Waggoner] not presented to you the words of the Bible? Why was it that I lost the manuscript and for two years could not find it? God has a purpose in this. *He wants us to go to the Bible and get the Scripture evidence.*" [19]

In this highly significant statement Ellen White realized God had purposed that her manuscript be lost to force the group to settle their questions from the

Bible alone. They were not to use her writings to interpret Scripture. She repeated this position some years later in the controversy over "the daily" in Daniel 8:11 (K.J.V.).[20]

Why the Need for Ellen White

If the Bible alone is enough, why does the church need Ellen White? "The written testimonies are not to give new light, but to impress vividly upon the heart the truths of inspiration already revealed. Man's duty to God and to his fellow man has been distinctly specified in God's word, yet but few of you are obedient to the light given."[21] "Little heed is given to the Bible, and the Lord has given a lesser light to lead men and women to the greater light."[22]

So God gave various spiritual gifts as lesser lights to lead His people to the greater light of Scripture. But these gifts are to be judged by the Word—never the other way around. During the historic Bible conferences of 1848, for example, Ellen White played a prime role in the formation of the Seventh-day Adventist Church's doctrinal platform. Each of the brethren had his own fervent interpretations. Unity seemed impossible. The deadlock broke when Ellen White was shown in vision the correct interpretations. How did this happen? Did they blindly accept her word as the word of God? Or did she clearly demonstrate *from Scripture* what was truth and on that basis win acceptance? The Bible was the answer for the pioneers. Nothing less could satisfy those noble men of God.

"Once Saved, Always Saved" for Prophets?

Some say that because Ellen White proved herself to be God's messenger in the 1840s, ever afterward everything she taught should be accepted as the word of God. But *there is no such thing as once saved, always saved, even for prophets.* Remember Baalam? Other examples are seen in Scripture where prophets wandered away from God's will (see 1 Kings 13). Ellen White, of course, remained faithful throughout her long ministry. Yet still, as a matter of principle we must test all her writings by the Word. At no point can we pronounce a prophet so faithful as to have outgrown the need of testing and to be in fact once saved, always saved.

Some would protest this testing process as presumption: "Are you saying I can pick and choose what is inspired and what isn't?" Of course we cannot pick and choose what we want from the Bible: "The Bible must not be interpreted to suit the ideas of men, however long they may have held these ideas to be true. We are not to accept the opinion of commentators as the voice of God; they were erring mortals like ourselves. God has given reasoning powers to us as well as to them. We should make the Bible its own expositor."[23]

What does the Bible say about last-day prophets? "Do not despise prophetic utterances. But examine everything carefully; hold fast to that which is good; abstain from every form of evil" (1 Thess. 5:20-22). Many are reluctant to perform this vital duty. It is difficult to examine truth for oneself. Our human nature finds it is so much easier to default on our responsibility and simply take everything the preacher or the prophet teaches as gospel. But the Word of God is clear—regarding "prophetic utterances," we must "examine *everything* carefully" and sift error from truth.

Time and place must always be considered. Since the messages mature with the movement, earlier writings may not reveal as much truth as later writings do. But we do not pick what we want and reject the rest. When the instruction of a preacher or prophet is validated by the Bible, we must pick up the cross even if it has splinters. We test by the Word and not by the flesh.

Remember the Bereans? Paul was a prophet, yet they did not accept anything he said without proving it for themselves by Scripture. Luke, the author of Acts, did not consider this doubting. He said they were noble (chap. 17:11).

More Than Pastoral Authority

What, then, is the authority of a prophet? Merely pastoral? No, much more. Pastors and teachers receive their instruction indirectly through the Bible. Prophets, on the other hand, receive direct inspiration from the Holy Spirit outside of the Written Word. One would expect a direct revelation from God through a vision to be more reliable and authoritative than an indirect revelation received through study, which must sift through one's background and prejudices. Yet both must be tested by the Bible. Both must be rejected if not in harmony with Scripture.

One of my former pastoral associates had been a missionary in Korea. He would be much more reliable and authoritative than I in translating that language. Why? I have only indirect access through an English-Korean dictionary; he had been in direct communication with Korea itself. Yet still his word is not final. Despite his expertise he may be mistaken. What he says must be tested by the dictionary—the same indirect revelation I must struggle with. Even so the prophet, despite direct revelation, must be proved by the Bible—unless you want confusion in the church.

If we fail to test Ellen White's messages by the Bible, what could prevent some new but false prophet from joining her in the circle of authority? This is the problem charismatics have. People jump up with messages "from the Lord" that contradict one another. How can you tell true from false? There must be a final authority above the gifts within the church.

Satan's Ingenious Deception

One of the most solemn warnings of inspiration is this: "The very last deception of Satan will be to make of none effect the testimony of the Spirit of God. . . . Satan will work ingeniously . . . to unsettle the confidence of God's remnant people in the true testimony." [24]

Is this ingenious deception happening right now? If so, how?

I see two basic attacks against Ellen White's authority. On the one hand, many despite her writings in order to do their own thing, speeding along "the highway to heaven" in reckless abandon. Will they be lost for rejecting Ellen White? Only because her straight testimony, which they refuse, is based upon the Bible. They will never see the pearly gates unless they humble themselves in harmony with Scripture.

False freedom is a dangerous temptation indeed. But Satan has reserved his most cunning deception for those who are sincerely obedient.

Have you ever heard this? "It's either all or nothing. If Ellen White is not 100 percent reliable she could not be from God. How could God inspire both truth and error?"

"All or nothing." This is the devil's ingenious deception. Many have forsaken the Bible, the Christian life, and the Adventist Church over the exaggerated expectation of "all or nothing." Were the Millerites perfect in their theology? Does the great Disappointment mean that God did not inspire their movement? How about John the Baptist? Then why Ellen White?

Satan's favorite way to undo is to overdo. A chilling example of this is the serpent's entrapment of Eve in Eden: "Eve had overstated the words of God's command. . . . She added the clause, 'Neither shall ye touch it, lest ye die' [K.J.V.] Here the subtlety of the serpent was seen. This statement of Eve gave him advantage, and he plucked the fruit, and placed it in her hand, and used her own words, 'He hath said, "If ye touch it, ye shall die." You see no harm comes to you from touching the fruit, neither will you receive any harm by eating it.' " [25]

Do you see it? Satan took Eve captive through overstating God's will. What ingenious deception! The devil has reserved this deadliest of tricks for such crucial moments of history. Why was Christ crucified? Because the Pharisees had overstated the restrictions of the Sabbath (see Mark 3:2-6). Messiah was murdered in the name of Moses. Satan destroyed the teaching of the prophet by overstating it. Has he done the same thing to Ellen White?

Notice this: Ten years before the just-quoted statement about Eve and the serpent, Ellen White incorrectly attributed Eve's words to God: "Of this tree *the Lord commanded* our first parents not to eat, *neither to touch it,* lest they die." [26]

Are you able to acknowledge this erroneous interpretation of the Bible by Ellen White? Do you have enough faith to look past her humanity and see the divine source of her gift? Or is your appreciation of inspiration so insecure that you must deceive yourself in order to retain your "faith"?

O God, help us! The very ones who fervently warn us not to be deceived are Satan's most effective instruments to destroy faith in Ellen White! Despite their sincerity. The tombstones of those who exaggerated the gift of prophecy line the hallway of Adventist history. Most defectors, from Dudley Canright to Walter Rea, have gone over the cliff because of disappointed expectations. How much pain we have suffered, how many souls have been lost, amid shattered illusions about inspiration. How many thousands have been turned away from Adventism because they could not accept unauthorized claims. How will their blood be accounted for? May God open our eyes before it is too late!

Let God Be God

Ellen White was always on the forward edge of marching truth. Throughout her ministry she uplifted Jesus her Friend according to the ever-increasing light shining upon her from heaven. Always she upheld the Bible. She is no more to blame for the abuse of the gift of prophecy than was Moses.

Where would the church be without her? Less enriched, for sure. But not lost. Some insist that Adventism will collapse unless its faith is built on her writings. Really? Is Ellen White the rock on which Christ built His church? When will we cease to dishonor her gift by such exaggeration? Which Adventist doctrine cannot stand on the Bible alone? How can Adventists expect fellow Christians to take them seriously until they are met on the solid rock of Scripture?

Much is being done these days to prove the integrity of Ellen White. Even lawyers have been hired to defend her honesty. But really she needs no defenders—she only needs to be read. Any genuine believer will recognize in her writings the voice of the Shepherd.

Yes, the Seventh-day Adventist Church is indeed a "prophet organization." And if we will let God be God and accept all His gifts on His terms, everything will be well with the church.

16 God's Heir-Born Remnant

F reedom and a fresh start. For three and a half centuries America has offered these priceless gifts of God to the poor and oppressed around the world. Under the Stars and Stripes you find the Kohlers and the Cohens, the Casarolis and the Kawolskis, the Cartwrights and the Castillos, the Kims and the Kirkwoods—all working together in peace and prosperity. Indeed, America is a salad bowl of nationalities. And religions.

With more denominations than a backslider has excuses, we are awash with worship. Everybody from African Methodists to Zen Buddhists is doing everything one can imagine for the Lord. There is snake handling for those who crave excitement, and padded pews if you would really rather watch today, thanks just the same. When a believer is bitten, faith healers to the rescue! And after their incantations fail, there is always baptism for the dead. No kidding.

Whatever you may want to do, you can probably do it in church. But which one? You would occupy every weekend for six years just in sampling each flavor of faith. Really, the choice is quite simple. The hundreds of denominations and cults branch out from five basic isms of religion. These are the great originals, leaders in unique and distinctive doctrine.

Atheism

Atheism, which denies anything supernatural, is actually the absence of religion. But in atheism's attempting natural explanations for the things of life, a philosophy has emerged that could be considered a counterfeit religion. For each of the great Christian truths, atheism offers an alternate: Creation? No, evolution. Afterlife? Nonsense! Only the here and now. Sin? Whatever you think it is. Salvation? From what? And so on.

Since ancient times atheism has infected religion. In Christ's day the Sadducees thought there was "no resurrection, nor an angel, nor a spirit" (Acts 23:8). Infidel ideas that sparked the eighteenth-century French Revolution have made startling inroads into major denominations today. A modified evolutionary theory is proposed that denies the six literal days of Creation. Miracles are considered quaint Jewish fables. Secular humanism has largely replaced Biblical brotherly love. Some ultraliberal groups, such as the Unitarian Universalists, are so influenced by atheistic concepts that they bear little resemblance to historic Christianity.

But even conservative Protestant seminaries have been infiltrated with subtle strains of atheism. Some of their freethinking scholars reject the Biblical atonement as a false concept. To them the law of God does not really exist, so there can be no penalty for its violation. This means that Christ's blood has no saving merit, that the cross was merely a piece of wood. Why did Jesus die? To show the universe His Father's wonderful love. God is too kind to punish and has no reason to, anyway. So literal hellfire is a myth. Hell is merely symbolic of God's sustaining life being withdrawn from sinners. By such deceptions atheism has influenced some liberal theologians in nearly every denomination to reject the ministration of Christ's blood in heaven—and the cleansing of the sanctuary from sin since 1844.

Paganism

Unlike atheism, which discredits anything supernatural, paganism acknowledges creative deity. Pagans believe that a spark of this divinity naturally indwells everyone. Salvation comes in developing this inherent deity. In this utter righteousness by works, pagans have no regard for either God's law or His blood, and reject the authority of the Judeo-Christian Bible. Many have their own scriptures, with a high moral code. Like the Indian leader Ghandi, pagans may be fervently devout, or grossly licentious like the ancient Canaanites and Corinthians. They can be sophisticated like the Greek philosophers or primitive like witch doctors. Their worship might involve the appeasement of demonic deities, the adoration of the sun god, or even the appreciation of an impersonal supreme force pervading all nature—pantheism, the heresy of John Harvey Kellogg, which the Adventist Church rejected at the turn of the century.

Catholicism

Rome rejects the pagan concept that man has inherent divinity. In harmony with other Christians, Catholics believe that grace is a free gift to helpless man through the blood of Jesus[1] and that Christians are called to obedience. But they believe that the death of Christ merely accesses the life-changing Spirit and cannot itself qualify anyone for heaven. Catholics find merit in the works of man done through the grace God imparts.[2] Their counterfeit sanctuary system is based on the transforming power of God's Spirit to make the saints worthy. This is legalism by faith.

A number of denominations called Protestant are really more like Catholics. While some, such as the Episcopalians, have obvious roots in Rome, others, like the Methodists, are harder to trace. Even though John Wesley shunned the ceremonies of Catholicism, surprisingly he taught somewhat the same brand of grace and salvation. From his misplaced confidence in sanctification, Wesley developed the "second blessing" baptism of the Holy Spirit, which led to the

Pentecostal holiness movement and indirectly the modern charismatic renewal. Because they find merit in the grace of God within through this extra "blessing" of the Spirit, Pentecostals subscribe to the Catholic mentality.

Interestingly, many groups who despise others' beliefs actually share the same basics. The Pharisees, for example, were horrified that their forefathers murdered the prophets—yet Jesus accused them of doing likewise. And Catholics decry the legalism of the Pharisees, yet indulge the same heresy. Pentecostals vigorously deny their Catholic connection because they reject its rituals—yet they cling to the same legalism by faith that those ceremonies represent.

Of course, we are making generalizations here. Denominations are classed together if they share the same underlying principles. There is much variance among churches of the same ism; some are not so radical as others. Even within a particular fellowship there can be extremes. For example, some conservative Jews are as legalistic as some Catholics, but the liberal wing in Judaism has been profoundly influenced by atheism. One thing is certain—if similar religious subgroups nailed a common roof over their beliefs, many members would be surprised who lived in neighboring apartments.

Calvinism

The Reformation broke away from Roman legalism, but also broke down. While restoring the blood of Christ as the only gateway to heaven, Calvin's passive faith drove him into the opposite ditch from papal legalism, radical predestination. This unfortunate doctrine proposes that God makes our choice for us whether or not we want to be saved. We have no free will to accept or reject the drawing of God's Spirit into salvation.[3]

By insisting that humans are not responsible for choosing salvation, Calvinism tends toward the neglect of God's law. When repentance is not essential in salvation it becomes optional.

Many today in the Reformed tradition may not go so far as Calvin did. But if they still retain his concept of passive faith and optional obedience, they are not being consistent in stopping short of radical predestination.

In summary so far, we have seen that atheism scoffs at anything supernatural. Paganism acknowledges some form of divinity but frankly rejects God's law and His blood. Catholicism finds merit through the law but denies the full meaning of the law. Calvinism recognizes the gateway to heaven but predetermines who will enter.

Every religious organization may be classed in one of these four categories, but for one—God's remnant, who honor His commandments through their faith in Jesus.

Adventism

Is it not somewhat pompous to consider the Advent Movement to be God's choice above all others? Careful analysis proves otherwise. Where else could God plant His truth? Certainly not in atheism or paganism. Nor in Catholicism and Calvinism, for both of them hold doctrines of alien origin. Following atheists, they deny the memorial of God's Creation, His Sabbath. They substitute the pagan day of sun worship, and also teach the natural immortality of the human soul. Though both Catholics and Calvinists worship God as Creator and deny inherent divinity within humanity, their theology expresses these non-Christian teachings anyway.

Misunderstanding man's state in death has opened communication with the spirit world of paganism and Christianized the monster of eternal punishment. Calvinists, who so much value Christ's blood, do not see that their concept of hell mocks Calvary. Think it through. If endless torture is the penalty of sin, then Jesus, who did not suffer eternally on the cross, did not pay the full price of sin.

In spurning the Sabbath and the mortality of man, Calvinists also refuse the sanctuary truth. While dismantling the counterfeit priesthood of Rome, they have resisted restoring the two-phase intercession of Christ's blood in the heavenly sanctuary.

Not only have Protestants failed to advance beyond their founders—they have even backslidden. An example of this is prophetic interpretation. The Reformers accused Rome of being the antichrist power. In their Counter-Reformàtion, Catholic scholars proposed opposing theories to the Protestant historicism—preterism and futurism. Protestants today are nearly all futurists or preterists. Those leaning toward Catholicism are futurists, and those inclined toward Calvinism are preterists. The truth about Christ's second coming has been buried in this further apostasy. And another bridge has been built for fellowship with Rome.

We have seen four pillars of truth trampled upon by each of the counterfeit isms: the Sabbath, life in Christ alone (mortal state of man), the sanctuary, and the Second Coming. God needs to restore all of them to His people.

He already has. These wonderful truths are the pillars of Adventism (with one more to be discussed shortly). Each is founded in the gospel as outlined in the three angels' messages of Revelation 14. The Sabbath calls us from our works to rest in Jesus Christ. Man's mortal state reminds us that our hope for eternal life is not in divinity within us, but outside of us in Christ. The sanctuary relieves anxiety about our sanctification by directing us away from ourselves to the throne of grace for righteousness. And the Second Coming reminds us that our blessed hope is Jesus Christ, not the baptism of another Pentecost.

We are humbled to realize that Adventism is the only denominational structure able to support true salvation by faith. Although there are many sincere followers of other isms, they are restricted from complete confession of Christ in the confines of their churches. Atheism, of course, rejects salvation entirely. Paganism finds a natural divinity that may be developed from within unto salvation. Catholics see nothing worthy within to begin with, until God infuses believers with the transforming grace of His Spirit. Calvinists find nothing worthy ever within man, who might be saved by God's will or damned in hell by that same sovereignty. Adventism finds nothing worthy ever within man, who will be saved if he trusts in Christ with faith that honors the holy law.

Only Adventism can bring true honor to the law and the blood. Atheism and paganism reject both openly; Catholicism and Calvinism annul both by their imbalance.

Also, Adventism is the one structure that can truly stand on the Bible alone. Atheists deny any supernatural inspiration. Pagans have only their heathen scriptures. Catholics reverence the Bible but drown in their tradition. Calvinists profess to abide by *sola Scriptura*—"the Bible only"—but their doctrinal pillars are shot through with paganism.

No Room for Pride

What a privilege to be entrusted with God's restoration of the Reformation! But before we Adventists go marching over the cliff in pride, we must take inventory. Has the church been faithful to its heritage of truth? If so, why is it still here? We could be rejoicing in the New Jerusalem, but instead are languishing in Laodicea. Being selfish and indolent, we are yet somehow proud of ourselves for possessing the pillars of truth.

Evidently we must yet learn the truth within the truth. We still have but shallow appreciation for the gospel within our pillars. Like the Pharisees, we are zealous Sabbatarians who have resisted Sabbath rest. We know where the dead are, but we have not been alive in Christ. We accept the sanctuary doctrine, but we ignore the daily intercession of our Priest. We talk of His soon return, yet we live as if He never will.

God attempted a breakthrough in 1888 with the truth as it is in Jesus. Through the ministry of Ellen White in the fifth pillar of Adventism—spiritual gifts—He sought to wake us up to the Word and keep us growing. Still we slumber. But the pillars remain, and because this is the only denomination that claims them, we are the fold God seeks to prepare for His sheep from Babylon. Enfeebled and defective though we be, we are still God's heir-born movement of destiny. But where do we go from here?

God's Blessings Are Conditional

History proves there is no "once saved, always saved" for individuals or denominations. The promises of God's eternal favor are transferable. The unbelieving Jews lost their promises to Christianity. After the apostasy came the Reformation, which likewise stalled out. Then Adventism appeared as God's heir-born remnant, inheriting the promises squandered by the others. Is the principle of conditional prophecy still valid? Did Jesus mean business when He threatened rejection of the Laodicean church? In 1888 "Mrs. White said that *if* the church should go into darkness *the Lord would raise up others to finish the work—that He had agents that He could call into action at any moment.*" [4]

How can Adventist destiny be preserved? To remain heir-born, our wings of faith must follow advancing truth. "But we received all our pillars of truth at the 1848 Bible conferences. Why should we need new light?" some may ask.

If you really wish to bed down with the pioneers, at what point would you like to dig in? In 1849, while they still believed in the shut door? Or in the legalism that reigned before 1888? Even at that Minneapolis Conference, Ellen White was "shown that Jesus will reveal to us *precious old truths in a new light,* if we are ready to receive them; *but they must be received in the very way in which the Lord shall choose to send them.*" [5]

The pillars remain the same, but we must increase in our understanding of them. *"No one must be permitted to close the avenues whereby the light of truth shall come to the people.* As soon as this shall be attempted, God's Spirit will be quenched, for that Spirit is constantly at work to give fresh and increased light to His people through His Word." [6]

After the Minneapolis Conference, Ellen White declared: "A spirit of pharisaism has been coming in upon the people who claim to believe the truth for these last days. They are self-satisfied. They have said, 'We have the truth. There is no more light for the people of God.' But we are not safe when we take a position that we will not accept anything else than that upon which we have settled as truth. We should take the Bible, and investigate it closely for ourselves." "There is no excuse for anyone in taking the position that there is no more truth to be revealed, and that all our expositions of Scripture are without an error. . . . There are those who oppose everything that is not in accordance with their own ideas, and by so doing they endanger their eternal interest as verily as did the Jewish nation in their rejection of Christ." "It was the unwillingness of the Jews to give up their long-established traditions that proved their ruin. They were determined not to see any flaw in their own opinions or in their expositions of the Scriptures. . . . We have many lessons to learn, and many, many to unlearn. God and heaven alone are infallible." [7]

So Adventists are heir-born—begotten of God to inherit the Reformation and complete it. The pillars when properly understood are pure and free from error. Heaven waits for us to discover the gospel foundation for the pillars. Truth demands change. But change is uncomfortable and frightening, since it disrupts our lives. We can invent all kinds of pious excuses for rejecting the gospel, but perhaps we are simply too lazy or scared to follow Jesus.

The Stage Is Being Set

As God is preparing His remnant fold to receive His sheep, the devil is setting up a den for his wolves—the ecumenical movement foretold by Revelation: "And I saw coming out of the mouth of the dragon and out of the mouth of the beast and out of the mouth of the false prophet, three unclean spirits like frogs; for they are spirits of demons, performing signs, which go out to the kings of the whole world, to gather them together for the war of the great day of God, the Almighty" (chap.

16:13, 14).

So the devil's all-star team will be the dragon, the beast, and the false prophet. These are the counterfeit isms, confederated against God's remnant. The dragon is paganism, with its outright connection with the devil (see chap. 12:9). The beast, of course, is Catholicism. The false prophet is Calvinism, which lays false claim to the Word of God in *sola Scriptura.*

What about atheism? Miracle-working evil spirits will gather together the leaders "of the whole world." Convinced by the satanic supershow, all atheists will be converted to counterfeit worship. Everyone but the remnant will be deceived or compelled to honor the beast and receive his mark.

The Charismatic Connection

Notice that these evil spirits will come out of the *mouths* of the unclean isms. What moves within a mouth? The tongue. And these spirits are described as froglike. What is the outstanding feature of a frog? His tongue. Could it be the tongues of a charismatic revival that will unite the world? Can it be anything else?

See how each of the four isms is vulnerable to a false Pentecost:

Atheists live by sight, not faith. Seeing is believing. They do not believe in God because they have not seen Him. No problem; the charismatic movement will work such miracles that the last doubter will be convinced into counterfeit worship.

Paganism speaks in tongues. Long before Pentecost, ancient heathen religions achieved union with their deities by means of charismatic ecstasy.[8] It is a chilling fact that modern satanism endorses speaking in tongues. The *Encyclopedia of Occultism and Parapsychology* devotes several pages to occult tongues, called "xenoglossis": "Speaking in an unknown language is a far more impressive phenomenon than writing in it. . . . In medieval times the speaking in foreign languages was one of the four principal signs of the presence of a demon."[9] Then this occult manual describes approvingly "how the gift descended on the congregation of Edward Irving in 1831."[10] According to this claim, Pentecostal tongues are a carryover from demon worship. Perhaps it was because of their pagan background that the Corinthian church went into error over unknown tongues (see 1 Corinthians 14).

Catholics claim the charismatic movement as God's answer to their prayer at the Vatican Council for a new Pentecost to revive and unify Christianity. Their obsession with perfection through receiving God's power within them makes them eager for the Pentecostal blessing.

There is also basic linkage between Calvinism and the charismatics. Although not quickly visible, it is deep. On the surface Calvinism is an objective religion (hope outside the believer), while the gospel of the charismatics is subjective (hope within the believer). But despite Calvinism's belief in Calvary's objective atonement, for everyday living it is definitely subjective—the elect are permitted to choose for themselves their own way and still be saved, not being tested by the law. So in daily practice both Calvinists and charismatics share a subjective religion.

There is another bridge of subjective belief that joins Calvinists with most charismatics—Sundaykeeping. Neither group believes one must enter God's rest to be saved. Calvinists believe the grace of God excuses one from any kind of necessary obedience, even the need to enter His chosen symbol of rest, the Sabbath. Most Pentecostals * reject Sabbath rest for a different reason—they ignore the finished work of Christ outside of us to focus on the working of the Spirit within us. Therefore Sunday, the Pentecostal power day, replaces the Sabbath of rest. Thus both groups join hands over Sunday, but for different reasons.

Both of them also share the rejection of God's law as a necessary standard. Charismatics talk much about obedience to the lordship of Christ and the importance of repentance. But they repent on their own terms, not God's—they have no use for the Ten Commandments. Why? The fourth calls them to rest in the accomplishments of Christ. Calvinism also does not consider that a willingness to repent from the transgression of God's law is a condition of salvation. So a common disregard for God's law provides a further tie to the charismatics for the Calvinists.

We have seen how the charismatic movement voids both respect for the law and rest in the blood by its subjective religion. But God's remnant, because they trust in the blood of Christ, "keep the commandments of God and their faith in Jesus" (Rev. 14:12). Through their freedom in faith they can obey. Only Adventism in Christ can respect both the law and the blood. All the other isms will eventually lead into contact with demons through counterfeit speaking in tongues.

Does this mean that charismatic Christians today are unsaved? Of course not, if they are truly committed to Christ. The disciples left all to follow Jesus, yet they still misunderstood the use of spiritual gifts. They wanted to call fire down from heaven to destroy unbelievers. Jesus did not question their salvation, but He informed them that a different spirit had control of them: " 'You do not know what kind of spirit you are of' " (Luke 9:55).

Our Adventist Destiny

As the world confederates under the banner of the beast, how thankful we Adventists can be for our treasures of truth. As each year goes by, my conviction deepens that God is preparing Adventism to be His movement of destiny.

Not long ago I conducted another evangelistic crusade. What a pleasure it was to preach our message again. Many of the guests came to us as already committed Christians. To watch them light up with increased appreciation of Jesus through our Adventist message thrilled and inspired my soul.

---

* There are several small Sabbatarian Pentecostal denominations.

But interestingly, most of those in my audiences were Adventists. I have noticed a hunger among our members for a deeper understanding of truth as it is in Jesus. On camp meeting tours, I have observed in our people the same burning yearning for learning and experiencing more of the peace and power of the gospel in the context of our mission and message.

What brings me the greatest joy is witnessing the rebirth of Adventism in the hearts of some who once bid us farewell. And they are being welcomed back with open arms!

So I feel good about our church. Some doomsayers predicted the funeral of Adventism. Instead, it is the offshoots that are fading away. God in His mercy has brought us through recent storms into position to venture forth as His heir-born remnant, proclaiming and preserving His pillars of truth.

Catholicism hopes vainly:

> "Just as I am, without one plea
> but that Thy love is seen in me."

Calvinism presumes brashly:

> "Just as I am, without one plea
> but that Thou hast fixed my destiny."

But Adventists may rest securely:

> "Just as I am, without one plea
> but that Thy blood was shed for me."

> O Lamb of God, we come!

ENDNOTES

Chapter Two

BIRTHDAY OF DESTINY

[1] LeRoy E. Froom, *The Prophetic Faith of Our Fathers* (Washington, D.C.: Review and Herald, 1954), Vol. IV, p. 463.

[2] *Ibid.*, pp. 466, 467.

[3] *Ibid.*, pp. 501, 502.

[4] Richard W. Schwarz, *Light Bearers to the Remnant* (Mountain View, Calif.: Pacific Press, 1979), p. 34.

[5] LeRoy E. Froom, *Movement of Destiny* (Washington, D.C.: Review and Herald, 1971), pp. 69, 70.

[6] *Ibid.*

[7] George Storrs, "Go Ye Out to Meet Him," *Bible Examiner*, Sept. 24, 1844, p. 2, in P. Gerard Damsteegt, *Foundations of the SDA Message and Mission* (Grand Rapids: William B. Eerdmans, 1977), p. 98.

[8] Froom, *The Prophetic Faith of Our Fathers*, Vol. IV, p. 855.

[9] Cited in Francis D. Nichol, *The Midnight Cry* (Washington, D.C.: Review and Herald, 1944), pp. 247, 248.

Chapter Three

JOY IN THE MORNING

[1] In Francis D. Nichol, *The Midnight Cry*, p. 458.

[2] Froom, *Movement of Destiny*, pp. 107-109.

[3] *Ibid.*, p. 86.

[4] Joseph Bates, *An Explanation of the Typical and Anti-Typical Sanctuary by the Scriptures* (New Bedford, Mass.: press of Benjamin Lindsey, 1850), p. 16.

[5] Robert W. Olson, *101 Questions on the Sanctuary and on Ellen White* (Washington, D.C.: Ellen G. White Estate, 1981), p. 58.

[6] *Ibid.*, p. 60.

[7] As the movement organized into a denomination in the 1860s, this concept of an investigative judgment ran as a common thread throughout official SDA publications.

[8] Miller himself related the judgment of Revelation 14 to the cleansing of the sanctuary mentioned in Daniel 8:14. Crosier connected the blotting out of sins with the cleansing of the ancient Day of Atonement. In 1850 Joseph Bates published the first clear statement of the investigative judgment doctrine. Three years later J. N. Andrews wrote a series on the subject, and 1854 brought additional features by J. N. Loughborough. Then Uriah Smith formally developed the idea of judgment with his special emphasis on the saints' being judged by books of record, resulting in the examination of individual character. (See "Investigative Judgment," *SDA Encyclopedia*, pp. 669-673.)

[9] Walter T. Rea, *The White Lie* (Turlock, Calif.: M & R Publications, 1982), p. 39.

[10] Froom, *op. cit.*, pp. 88, 89.

[11] Ellen G. White manuscript 5, 1889; quoted in Robert J. Wieland, *The 1888 Message* (Nashville: Southern Publishing, 1980), p. 51.

Chapter Four

THE SOLUTION FOR "SADVENTISM"

[1] Walter R. Martin, *The Kingdom of the Cults* (Minneapolis: Bethany House, 1965), p. 406. Dr. Martin has enjoyed much friendly discussion with Adventist leaders and has defended Adventists from those who consider the church a cult.

[2] "Judged" is from the same root as the noun *krisis*, in its verb form *krinō*, which translated means "to judge or

119

decide."

³ Note the timing of this judgment. Christ will not come until after the close of the gospel proclamation (see Matt. 24:14). Since this judgment accompanies the preaching of the gospel, it must precede the return of Jesus—a pre-Advent judgment.

⁴ "Evangelical" Adventist—many Adventists who minimize or discard doctrines of the church not in harmony with their understanding of the gospel use this term to identify themselves.

⁵ Ellen White, *The Great Controversy* (Mountain View, Calif.: Pacific Press, 1888), p. vii.

⁶ Isidore Singer, ed., *The Jewish Encyclopedia* (New York: Funk & Wagnalls, 1904), Vol. II, p. 293.

⁷ *Ibid.*

⁸ W. M. Chandler, *The Trial of Jesus*, vol. 1, pp. 153, 154, in Taylor G. Bunch, *"Behold the Man!"* (Nashville: Southern Publishing, 1946), p. 66.

⁹ Bunch, *op. cit.*, p. 64.

¹⁰ Singer, Vol. II, p. 294.

¹¹ *Ibid.*, Vol. X, p. 204. The Father gave Jesus " 'authority to execute judgment, because He is the Son of Man' " (John 5:27). Both Father and Son work together to defend us, so both are considered our judge (cf. Heb. 12:23, 24 with Acts 10:40-42). Both are also called Saviour (Titus 1:3, 4) and Creator (cf. Mark 13:19 with John 1:3). All three members of the Godhead work in concert.

¹² Now we may see harmony between 2 Corinthians 5:10 and John 5:24.

¹³ Various texts that reveal the interest celestial beings have in God's work to save humanity are 1 Peter 1:12; Exodus 25:20; Ephesians 3:10; 1 Corinthians 4:9.

Chapter Five

THE RISE AND FALL OF ANTICHRIST

¹ H. Grattan Guinness, *Romanism and the Reformation* (Boston: Arnold Publishing, 1890), pp. 41, 42, in Desmond Ford, *Daniel*, (Nashville: Southern Publishing, 1978), p. 151.

² See chart by William H. Shea, in *Daniel and the Judgment* (Washington, D.C.: Biblical Research Institute of the General Conference of Seventh-day Adventists, 1980), p. 42.

³ "Preterism teaches that all Biblical prophecy must find its fulfillment within either the lifetime of the prophet or within near proximity; thus, prophecy has its primary meaning only for the contemporaries of the prophet."— W. H. Johns, *The ABC's of Desmond Ford's Theology* (Washington, D.C.: SDA Biblical Research Institute), p. 2.

⁴ See Froom, *The Prophetic Faith of Our Fathers*, Vol. II, pp. 486-512.

⁵ Arthur J. Ferch, "The Judgment Scene in Daniel 7," in Arnold V. Wallenkampf, ed., *The Sanctuary and the Atonement* (Washington, D.C.: Review and Herald, 1981), p. 160.

⁶ Johns, *op. cit.*, p. 16.

⁷ "True, there was a Median empire preceding the Persian, but it had been conquered by Cyrus some years before his conquest of Babylon. Hence it is historically impossible for it to be the second of the four kingdoms, following Babylon. Neither does the book of Daniel separate Median from Persian rule. The Babylonian kingdom is replaced by that of 'the Medes and Persians' (Dan. 5:28); Darius the Mede enforces the laws of 'the Medes and Persians' (Dan. 6:12); the combined rule of 'Media and Persia'—symbolized by the single ram (Dan. 8:20)—is destroyed and replaced by the Grecian goat."—*Seventh-day Adventists Answer Questions on Doctrine* (Washington, D.C.: Review and Herald, 1957), p. 323.

Others seek to divide the third empire, Greece, into two kingdoms by separating Alexander the Great's empire from his successors. But "Alexander's successors did not constitute a distinct kingdom that replaced its predecessors by conquest, as did the others; it was merely a continuation and development out of Alexander's rule. But in Daniel 2 and 7 the fourth kingdom is not a later phase of the third; it is as distinct as the other three. Not only is the fourth beast separate, but it is even 'diverse' [K.J.V.] from its predecessors. A Hellenistic fourth kingdom does not fit the specifications."—*Ibid.*, pp. 322, 323.

Incidently, "the origin of the Greek fourth kingdom is generally credited, not to a Christian exegete, but to a pagan, Porphyry, who died about A.D. 304. It was devised, not to expound, but to discredit and deny the prophetic element of the book of Daniel."—*Ibid.*, p. 320.

⁸ *Ibid.*

⁹ H.D.M. Spence and J. S. Exell, eds., *The Pulpit Commentary* (New York: Funk & Wagnalls, 1950), vol. 29, p. 218.

¹⁰ C. Mervin Maxwell, *God Cares* (Mountain View, Calif.: Pacific Press, 1981), vol. 1, p. 154.

¹¹ See Shea, *op. cit.*, p. 54.

¹² See chart in Froom, *op. cit.*, p. 528.

¹³ *Ibid.*, p. 784.

¹⁴ *Ibid.*

¹⁵ *Ibid.*, Vol. III, p. 252.

¹⁶ Guinness, in Ford, *op. cit.*, pp. 42, 43, *loc. cit.*

¹⁷ Froom, *op. cit.*, Vol. I, p. 713.

¹⁸ *Ibid.*, Vol. II, pp. 528, 784.

¹⁹ Ford, *op. cit.*, p. 154. In fairness to Dr. Ford, we must note that this 1978 defense of Adventist doctrine does not represent his present position.

²⁰ Edward Heppenstall, *Our High Priest* (Washington, D.C.: Review and Herald, 1972), p. 110.

Chapter Six

THE DILEMMA OF DANIEL 8

[1] Maxwell, *God Cares*, vol. 1, p. 153.

[2] *Ibid.*

[3] *Questions on Doctrine*, p. 328.

[4] In contesting this interpretation, one scholar contends that "a Hebrew reader could not possibly understand the period of time 2300 evening-mornings of 2300 half days or 1150 whole days, because evening and morning at the creation constituted not the half but the whole day. . . . We must therefore take the words as they are, *i.e.* understand them of 2300 whole days."—C. F. Keil, *Biblical Commentary on the Book of Daniel* (Grand Rapids: William B. Eerdmans, 1975), pp. 303, 304, in Ford, *Daniel*, p. 197.

[5] Another theologian insists that "using the figure of eleven hundred and fifty days only creates more problems as it does not fit precisely any scheme of events and has a dubious base."—John F. Walvoord, *Daniel: The Key to Prophetic Revelation* (Chicago: Moody Press, 1971), p. 190. For additional refutation of the division into 1150 days, see Maxwell, *op. cit.*, pp. 173, 174.

[6] Ford, *op. cit.*, p. 164.

[7] *Questions on Doctrine*, p. 260.

[8] Maxwell, *op. cit.*, p. 155. Rome "grew exceedingly great" "out of one of them" (verse 9), that is, out of one of "the four winds of heaven" in verse 8. Some suggest that the little horn must emerge from among the four horns of the Greek Empire, not from the four winds. But pronouns must agree in gender with their antecedent nouns. "In the Hebrew for Daniel 8:8, 9, 'horns' is feminine, and 'winds' is either masculine or feminine. In the phrase 'out of one of them,' the pronoun 'them' is masculine. This means that the antecedent noun for 'them' cannot be 'horns' but must be 'winds.' . . . It was to arise from one of the four directions of the compass."—*Ibid.*, p. 152.

[9] Harry A. Dawe, *Ancient Greece and Rome: World Cultures in Perspective* (Columbus, Ohio: Charles E. Merrill, 1970), p. 188.

[10] Ford, *op. cit.*, p. 192.

[11] Maxwell, *op. cit.*, p. 155.

[12] Baltimore Catechism, sec. 360, in Maxwell, *op. cit.*, p. 167.

[13] Shea, *Daniel and the Judgment*, p. 409. Gerhard Hasel proposes: "It appears that the ideas of 'cleansing,' 'justifying,' 'setting right,' and 'vindicating' are part and parcel of the term 'nisdaq.' Unfortunately, there does not seem to be a single word in the English language that captures these primary semantic connotations. All in all, this means that the 'cleansing' of the sanctuary is to be seen in a broader scope, inclusive of ideas of restoration to a rightful state—cleansing, justification, and vindication."—"The 'Little Horn,' the Saints, and the Sanctuary in Daniel 8," *Sanctuary*, p. 204.

[14] Shea, *op. cit.*, pp. 409, 410.

[15] Heppenstall, "The Pre-Advent Judgment," *Ministry*, December, 1981, p. 15.

[16] Ford, *op. cit.*, p. 189.

Chapter Seven

WORTH ITS WAIT IN GOLD

[1] In Ford, *Daniel*, p. 198. Newton was specifically describing verses 24-27.

[2] The years 605-538 B.C., counted inclusively. See Maxwell, *God Cares*, vol. 1, p. 190.

[3] Shea believes that Daniel 9 came "a decade later" than Daniel 8 ("The Relationship Between the Prophecies of Daniel 8 and Daniel 9," in Wallenkampf, ed., *The Sanctuary and the Atonement*, p. 240). Maxwell sees thirteen years (*op. cit.*, p. 189).

[4] Note the transition from Daniel 9:2 to verse 3.

[5] *The SDA Bible Commentary* (Washington, D.C.: Review and Herald, 1977), vol. 4, p. 852.

[6] Shea, *Daniel and the Judgment*, p. 71.

[7] *The New Brown, Driver, and Briggs Hebrew and English Lexicon* (Lafayette, Ind.: Associated Publishers, 1981), p. 1070.

[8] *The Pulpit Commentary*, vol. 29, p. 267.

[9] Shea, *op. cit.*, p. 73.

[10] Joyce G. Baldwin, *Daniel*, Tyndale Old Testament Commentaries (Downers Grove, Ill.: Inter-Varsity Press, 1978), p. 169.

[11] Shea, *loc. cit.*

[12] Literal meaning of Daniel 9:24, as noted in margin of the *New American Standard Bible*.

[13] Ford, *op. cit.*, p. 227.

[14] Shea, *op. cit.*, pp. 74, 75.

[15] *Ibid.*, pp. 372, 373.

[16] "The Hebrew expression employed applies to things rather than persons."—Ford, *loc. cit.* Heppenstall observes that "the Hebrew expression used here for 'most holy' is qodesh qodashîm, the plural form meaning 'holy places.' . . . The phrase occurs forty-four times in the Old Testament and refers everywhere to the place of the sanctuary, and not to a person or persons. 1 Chronicles 23:13 is regarded as the one exception. But it is poor exegesis

to adopt the one doubtful use that differs from the other forty-three uses as a basis to say this phrase in Daniel refers to the person of Christ."—Heppenstall, *Our High Priest*, p. 151.

[17] Shea, *op. cit.*, p. 75. Maxwell notes that "the word 'place' is not used in the *original* language of Daniel 9:24. In the Bible many things associated with the sanctuary are called 'most holy,' including the altar of burnt offering (Exodus 29:37), the golden altar (Exodus 30:10), sin offerings (Leviticus 6:29), and incense (Exodus 30:36)."—Maxwell, *op. cit.*, p. 208. Therefore this anointing involves the heavenly sanctuary as a whole.

[18] Heppenstall, *loc. cit.*

[19] *Ibid.*

[20] "The evidence is overwhelming that the New Testament teaches that [Daniel] 9:24-27 was *not* accomplished in the days of Antiochus Epiphanes," asserted Desmond Ford in 1978 *(Daniel, p. 207)*.

Chapter Eight

FAREWELL, ADVENTISM?

[1] Maxwell, *God Cares*, vol. 1, pp. 200, 201.
[2] *Ibid.*, p. 201.
[3] Robert D. Brinsmead, *Judged by the Gospel* (Fallbrook, Calif.: Verdict Publications, 1980), pp. 86, 87.
[4] See *Questions on Doctrine*, p. 295.
[5] Gleason L. Archer, *Encyclopedia of Bible Difficulties* (Grand Rapids: Zondervan, 1982), p. 290.
[6] Gerhard F. Hasel, "The Seventy Weeks of Daniel 9:24-27," insert in *Ministry*, May, 1976, p. 14-D.
[7] Maxwell, *op. cit.*, p. 202.
[8] See Siegfried H. Horn, "Elephantine Papyri and Daniel 8:14," *Ministry*, August, 1981, pp. 24-27.
[9] See Hasel, *op. cit.*, p. 20-D, note 133.
[10] Ford, *Daniel*, p. 214.
[11] *Questions on Doctrine*, p. 276. For an example of this see Genesis 29:27.
[12] Hasel, *op. cit.*, p. 5-D.
[13] *American Heritage Dictionary* (Boston: Houghton Mifflin, 1981), p. 615.
[14] Archer, *op. cit.*, pp. 290, 291.
[15] See marginal note on Daniel 9:25, N.A.S.B.
[16] Maxwell, *op. cit.*, p. 217.
[17] *Ibid.*, p. 218.
[18] *Ibid.*, p. 255.
[19] *Ibid.*, p. 218.

Chapter Nine

ROOTS OF THE HOLOCAUST

[1] Shea, *Daniel and the Judgment*, p. 268.
[2] Ford, *Daniel*, p. 228.
[3] *Questions on Doctrine*, pp. 293, 295.
[4] Baldwin, *Daniel*, pp. 176, 177.
[5] Raymond H. Woolsey, *The Power and the Glory* (Washington, D.C.: Review and Herald, 1978), pp. 44, 45.
[6] *Questions on Doctrine*, pp. 299, 300.
[7] Mark Finley class lecture on Daniel for the Andrews University Seminary Extension at Hinsdale, Illinois, March 6, 1980.
[8] *Questions on Doctrine*, p. 301.
[9] *Ministry*, October, 1980, p. 38.
[10] Ford, *op. cit.*, p. 207.
[11] *Ibid.*, p. 225.
[12] *The Pulpit Commentary*, vol. 29, p. 267.
[13] Jacques Doukhan, "The Seventy Weeks of Daniel 9: An Exegetical Study," in Wallenkampf, ed., *The Sanctuary and the Atonement*, p. 270, note 11.
[14] *Ibid.*, p. 255.
[15] Woolsey, *op. cit.*, p. 45.
[16] *Questions on Doctrine*, p. 277.
[17] *Ibid.*, p. 309.
[18] *Ibid.*, p. 310.
[19] *Ibid.*, p. 311.
[20] *Ibid.*, p. 312.
[21] Froom, *The Prophetic Faith of Our Fathers*, Vol. II, pp. 687, 688.
[22] *Questions on Doctrine*, p. 313.
[23] *Ibid.*, pp. 315, 316.

Chapter Ten

MYSTERY OF THE FIRST CENTURY

[1] This manuscript of nearly a thousand pages was prepared especially to be studied by the Sanctuary Review Committee, an officially authorized group of Adventist administrators, theologians, and pastors that convened during the summer of 1980 at Glacier View Camp, Ward, Colorado.

[2] Desmond Ford, *Daniel 8:14, the Day of Atonement, and the Investigative Judgment* (Casselberry, Fla.: Evangelion Press, 1980), p. 215. This is the manuscript cited in the preceding note, now published in book form by the author.

[3] Johns, *The ABC's of Desmond Ford's Theology*, p. 8.

[4] *Ibid.*, p. 10.

[5] *Ibid.*, p. 11.

[6] *Ibid.*

[7] *Ibid.*, p. 12.

[8] *Ministry*, October, 1980, p. 32.

[9] Ford, *Daniel*, p. 302.

[10] *Ibid.*, pp. 302, 303.

[11] William Shea, "The Year-Day Principle in Prophecy," *Pacific Union Recorder*, Sept. 22, 1980, p. 2.

[12] *Ibid.*

[13] See note 1 of this chapter.

[14] *Ministry*, October, 1980, p. 17.

[15] *The SDA Bible Commentary*, vol. 7, p. 729.

[16] *Ibid.*, vol. 4, pp. 29, 30.

[17] *Ibid.*, pp. 729, 730. (Italics supplied.)

[18] Doubters of God's ability to foretell human decisions should realize that history proves otherwise. God knew beforehand, for example, that if David had stayed in the city of Keilah, Saul would have hunted for him, and the citizens would have cooperated. David heeded the warning and escaped. (See 1 Sam. 23:9-13.) Many more examples could be given that God knows everything, " 'declaring the end from the beginning and from ancient times things which have not been done, saying, "My purpose will be established, and I will accomplish all My good pleasure" ' " (Isa. 46:10). God foretold to the very day when His people would be freed from Egypt (Ex. 12:40, 41). He knew beforehand that the Persian king Cyrus would be good to His people (Isa. 44:28-45:3). Christ even foresaw the taxpaying fish (Matt. 17:24-27), and the noisy rooster that would rebuke His thrice-erring disciple (Mark 14:29-31).

Chapter Eleven

CLEAN BEFORE THE LORD

[1] *Ministry*, October, 1980, p. 18.

[2] *Ibid.*

[3] *Ibid.*

[4] *Ibid.*, p. 35.

[5] *The New Brown, Driver, and Briggs Hebrew and English Lexicon*, p. 497.

[6] See *Questions on Doctrine*, p. 341.

[7] Heppenstall, *Our High Priest*, p. 25.

[8] Verses 20, 26, and 35 of Leviticus 4 provide additional evidence that the daily service involved atonement.

[9] Azazel as the devil is abundantly documented in *Questions on Doctrine*, pp. 391-395.

[10] White, *The Great Controversy* (Mountain View, Calif.: Pacific Press, 1911), p. 678.

[11] Heppenstall, *op. cit.*, p. 95.

Chapter Twelve

WHEN FREEDOM REIGNS

[1] Charles H. Spurgeon, quoted in Al Fasol, *Selected Readings in Preaching* (Grand Rapids: Baker Book House, 1980), in Robert Brinsmead, *What Is the Gospel?* (Fallbrook, Calif.: Verdict Publications, 1981), p. 2.

[2] Ellen White agonized to correct this abuse of the gospel in 1888 at the Minneapolis General Conference session. For a background of this struggle, see Froom, *Movement of Destiny*.

[3] Those who insist upon "once saved, always saved" should realize that Christ means what He says here.

[4] Similar acclaims to God's kingdom and character follow the Revelation 4 and 5 judgment throughout the book. See chaps. 11:17; 12:10; 14:7; 15:3, 4; 16:5-7; 18:20; 19:1-7.

[5] Throughout Revelation, as God conducts and executes judgment, Day of Atonement imagery is dominant. In chapter 8, for example, an "angel came and stood at the altar, holding a golden censer; and much incense was given to him, that he might add it to the prayers of all the saints upon the golden altar which was before the throne" (verse 3). Extra incense filled the censer on the Day of Atonement, symbolizing total dependence upon the merits of Jesus in judgment.

Chapter Thirteen

A VEILED THREAT

[1] *Ministry*, October, 1980, p. 48.

[2] Remember Numbers 28:30, for example. Chapter eleven of this book reviewed the doctrine of atonement in some depth.

[3] Bulls are different from calves. "There is a linguistic distinction between 'goats and calves,' and 'goats and bulls.'"—*Ministry*, October, 1980, p. 50. Bulls were sacrificed many times throughout the year, *not only* on the Day of Atonement. So their use on Yom Kippur proves nothing. A calf was sacrificed on inauguration day, *not at all* on the Day of Atonement. So the mention of calves in Hebrews 9:12 proves that Yom Kippur is *not* under discussion in this passage.

[4] Fritz Guy, *The Ministry of Christ as High Priest in Heaven: Some Suggestions Toward a Theology of the Sanctuary* (Berrien Springs, Mich.: Andrews University, 1980), p. 20.

[5] "It is a striking fact that the same verb *katharizō* is used in the Septuagint [Greek Old Testament] translation of Leviticus 16:19, 20, 30, *i.e.*, texts speaking of the cleansing of the sanctuary on the Day of Atonement."—Gerhard F. Hasel, *Christ's Atoning Ministry in Heaven*, (Leominster, Mass.: Eusey Press, n.d.), p. 25C.

[6] *Ministry*, October, 1980, p. 51.

[7] Guy, *op. cit.*, p. 18.

[8] *Ministry*, October, 1980, p. 21.

[9] Ford, *Daniel 8:14, the Day of Atonement, and the Investigative Judgment*, ms. p. A-60, in *Ministry*, October, 1980, p. 52.

[10] *Ministry*, October, 1980, p. 52.

[11] Ford, *op. cit.*, p. 2.

[12] William G. Johnsson, *In Absolute Confidence* (Nashville: Southern Publishing, 1979), p. 116.

[13] ———, "The Significance of the Day of Atonement Allusions in the Epistle to the Hebrews," in Wallenkampf, ed., *The Sanctuary and the Atonement*, p. 389.

[14] M. L. Andreasen, *The Sanctuary Service* (Washington, D.C.: Review and Herald, 1969), p. 218.

[15] *Ibid.*, p. 220.

[16] Ford, *op. cit.*, p. 1.

Chapter Fourteen

SABBATH WREST

[1] Kevin Phillips, "Has American Religion Begun Its Fourth Great Awakening?" Los Angeles *Herald Examiner*, April 17, 1981, p. A-15. This major survey was commissioned by Connecticut Mutual Life Insurance.

[2] *Ibid.* (Italics supplied.)

[3] Luke Connaughton, *A-Z of the Catholic Church* (Leigh-on-Sea, Essex, England: Kevin Mayhew Publishers, 1980), p. 37.

[4] Russell Chandler, "Charismatics Gain Pope's Approval; Controversial Catholic Movement Blessed During Pentecost," Los Angeles *Times*, June 8, 1975.

[5] Connaughton, *loc. cit.*

[6] Edward O'Connor, *The Pentecostal Movement in the Catholic Church* (Notre Dame, Ind.: Ave Maria Press, 1971), p. 28. O'Connor continues on page 183: "The spiritual experience of those who have been touched by the grace of the Holy Spirit in the Pentecostal movement is in profound harmony with the classical spiritual theology of the Church." Cited in a special issue of *Present Truth*.

[7] Christian Action Council, "The CAC: Standing in the Gap" (788 National Press Building, Washington, D.C.). The quotation continues by stating CAC's purpose: to exhibit God's compassion to "those who want to obey God." This only raises questions: Who defines obedience to God? And what should the state do with those who do not want to obey God?

[8] *Commonweal*, Oct. 9, 1981, in *Undercurrent*, vol. 15, No. 4.

[9] *Moral Majority Report*, April 20, 1981, in *Undercurrent*, vol. 15, No. 2.

[10] *Ibid.*

[11] *The New Brown, Driver, and Briggs Hebrew and English Lexicon*, p. 991.

[12] John A. O'Brien, *The Faith of Millions* (Huntington, Ind.: Our Sunday Visitor, 1974), p. 400.

[13] *New Catholic Encyclopedia* (New York: McGraw-Hill, 1967), Vol. XIII, p. 797.

Chapter Fifteen

A NONPROPHET ORGANIZATION

[1] Froom, *Movement of Destiny*, p. 241.

[2] Ellen White, in *Review and Herald*, March 11, 1890.

[3] In Froom, *op. cit.*, p. 228.